CHOICES

CHOICES
THE SHEEP GATE

Brian Horst

Tampa, Florida

The views and opinions expressed in this book are solely those of the author and do not reflect the views or opinions of Gatekeeper Press. Gatekeeper Press is not to be held responsible for and expressly disclaims responsibility for the content herein.

CHOICES:
The Sheep Gate

Published by Gatekeeper Press
7853 Gunn Hwy., Suite 209
Tampa, FL 33626
www.GatekeeperPress.com

Copyright © 2023 by Brian Horst

All rights reserved. Neither this book, nor any parts within it may be sold or reproduced in any form or by any electronic or mechanical means, including information storage and retrieval systems, without permission in writing from the author. The only exception is by a reviewer, who may quote short excerpts in a review.

Author photo taken by Sheila Hoover
Front cover image by IStock by Getty Images

Library of Congress Control Number: 2023942538

ISBN (hardcover): 9781662940323
ISBN (paperback): 9781662940330
eISBN: 9781662940347

Contents

Life	1
How and Why	15
React and Respond	25
God	41
Plagues	55
Commandments	81
Gates	99
The Ten Tens	121

Life

What is this crazy thing we call life? It makes no sense. Why am I here? I didn't ask to be born. I don't know what I'm doing here, but I'm trying to get through it. Most of the time, I feel like I did something wrong. The rest of the time, someone is telling me how bad I am, even though they don't seem to be doing much better than I am. I constantly wonder if this is even real. Maybe I'm just dreaming or stuck in some deep coma? I need help. I'm stuck. I feel lost. Like I'm running in some deep, dark woods and the batteries in my flashlight are running out. I have no idea how much time I have left here. I'm trying, I'm failing, and I'm not far from giving up. Why should I even bother doing this? None of it makes any sense. What's my next step?

Those are my own questions, but we've all had questions similar to those. This life is a challenge, and not a single one of us has asked to be born. And not a single one of us has been given instructions on how to live this life. Our only guides are people older than us, who barely know what they're doing. The only guides they

CHOICES

had were people older than them, who barely knew what they were doing. All of us are trying to figure out this thing called life and how to get through it. But all of us make mistakes and bad choices. Or in other words, all of us fail. But we also notice how many mistakes and bad choices others make. That helps us feel a little better about our own lives. We think that as long as other people have more problems than we do, we mustn't be doing too badly. And as long as we try to live a good life, we'll be fine, right?

We believe everything will work out if you make the right choices, treat others respectfully, and never give up. But do any of us honestly believe that, or are we trying to convince ourselves that that's right? We have a hard time accomplishing those things. We constantly make the wrong choices, yell at people in traffic, and give up on projects. The question is, why? Why is it so easy to do these things we know we shouldn't do? Why is it so easy to put others down and realize their stupidity? Why is it so easy to give up on yourself? Why is it so easy to live this life like you're almost dead?

What is life? The simple answer to that question is that life is choices. Every single moment of every single day, you are making a choice. As soon as you wake up, you have to make the choice to either get out of bed or go back to sleep. Some of you think that that isn't a choice because you have to get up every morning and face responsibility. You might have to go to work to support yourself and your family if you have a family. But believe it or not, it is still a choice. Part of that choice is being responsible. Some of you might have to wake up to care for a child or a parent or feed your pet. Whatever your reason, it is because you are being responsible. Something in your life needs to be taken care of, and you are choosing to take care of it. Whether that is yourself, a pet, an older person—or nine kids, a wife, and three dogs—it is all being responsible. You are responsible for every choice you make, every action you take, and every word you say. What does the word *responsible* actually mean? One definition is "being the primary cause of something and so able to be blamed or credited for it." Another definition says "involving important duties, independent decision-making, or control over others." (Source: Oxford languages)

Would you agree that you are the primary cause of every action you make and every word you say? Are you also involved in important duties—such as going to a job, doing housework, raising kids, or possibly all three? Do you make independent decisions, such as "I'm going to take a shower today" or "I'm going to feed my baby"? Do you have any control over others, such as a child, an employee, a spouse, a sibling, or a pet? That doesn't mean you are in total control. But there are parts of their life you have some control over. Every one of us can answer yes to these questions as long as we are not mentally challenged or handicapped in some way.

Now the question is, why? Why do we have so many choices to make and so many responsibilities? How can we possibly make the right choices when we are constantly making choices? "Should I eat broccoli today instead of a hot dog, and can I put cheese sauce on it?" "Should I wear a button-down shirt, or will a T-shirt be okay—it's only a funeral?" "Is it a bad idea to try to jump off my garage, hit the trampoline, and try to make it into the swimming pool?"

CHOICES

Those are only examples, but they aren't even close to what goes through our heads in one day. We have many different choices to make. We get all kinds of ideas, we come up with all sorts of crazy ways to accomplish our ideas and goals, and our thought life never shuts off. We can have a full-blown conversation with someone while thinking about how we want to build a ramp for our child so they can jump off their bike in midair. We may not hear a single word they say during the conversation, but we can pretend pretty well until they ask a question, then we are in trouble. But how does all this work, and where do our thoughts come from?

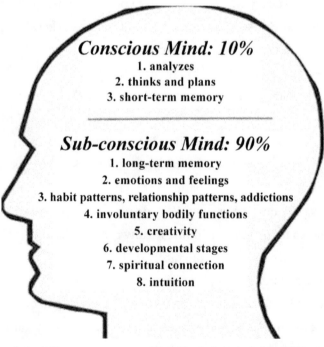

(Source: https://www.quora.com/How-do-I-change-subconscious-habits)

LIFE

There are two main parts to our mind, our conscious and subconscious. Our subconscious mind controls 90 percent of our life. Our subconscious mind includes our beliefs, attitudes, feelings, emotions, and memories. And it controls our involuntary body functions. Those are things like breathing, digestion, blinking—all those things we don't realize we do but would die or become very ill if we didn't do them. Our subconscious is formed just before our birth. If it weren't, we would die before we had a chance to live. Without our subconscious mind we would never start to breathe. Think about that: you control all your bodily functions but don't realize you're doing it because your subconscious mind does it for you. That's one responsibility you don't have to worry about.

Our subconscious mind is all that we run on from birth until roughly the age of six. There isn't an exact age, but we develop our conscious mind somewhere around six. Our conscious mind is our thoughts and reasoning. Right now you are most likely thinking about the conscious and subconscious mind, having a thought. Trying to understand what they do and how they work, weighing the differences, is reasoning. When we have a thought, we can look at it from many different angles and consider all the options. We can reason why this is a good or bad idea and gain a complete understanding of it. But our subconscious mind is what influences our conscious mind. All our reasoning comes from past experiences, and past experiences form our beliefs, attitudes, feelings, and emotions about everything we think about. Our subconscious mind stores all our memories, and our conscious mind stores our short-

CHOICES

term memories. We will take this step-by-step so that it's easier to understand. All this can get confusing very quickly.

When you are born, you rely entirely on your parents or whoever is raising you. They have to do everything for you. You can't do anything for yourself. Your subconscious is all you are running on, and mainly it's operating all your bodily functions. As your brain develops and you grow physically, you learn how to roll over and squirm around. Then you can find toys and other things to play with. As soon as you can move from one spot to another, you start to get into trouble. You put things into your mouth, touch stuff you shouldn't touch, roll and squirm into places you aren't supposed to be, and become very curious. But as a baby, there are no long-lasting mental consequences for your choices, good or bad. It's just something you did. There can be long-lasting physical consequences.

But your brain hasn't developed enough for you to understand right and wrong, or reward and punishment. You can't learn anything because you haven't developed a conscious mind, which gives you the ability to think and reason. You are just doing whatever you are doing, and there are no thoughts about it. That means you are innocent. As a child, you are innocent or blameless. That means you are free from guilt and sin, primarily through the lack of the understanding of evil. Having the understanding of something is gained through experience or association. If you don't know or can't learn what good and evil or right and wrong are, you can't be guilty of doing them. You don't understand what they are.

LIFE

We are born with evil intentions inside us. We have the knowledge of both good and evil inside of us when we are born, but we don't understand either of them. If we weren't born with the knowledge of evil, we wouldn't hit other kids or steal their toys. Just like if we weren't born with the knowledge of good, we wouldn't give a toy to another child or help them up when they fall. But we don't understand our actions or what they are; they're just something we do.

As a small child, you are still innocent, but you begin to learn right and wrong and reward and punishment. You still don't fully understand them, but you may start to have some responsibilities at this point in life. Adults may tell you to pick up your toys and be nice to your siblings and other children. If you do that, your parents, or whoever is raising you, will be at least happy you did it. They may even get you a new toy or some ice cream. If you don't do it, at the very least, your parents, or whoever is raising you, will be upset with you. They may even take something from you.

These are just examples. Everyone's experience growing up is different. But when we have consequences for the things we do and the things we say, we begin to learn. Things like picking up our toys are responsibilities. As soon as we have responsibilities, we don't want to do them and can be better at keeping up with them. For example, most children need to be told by an adult to clean up their toys before they do it. And even then, they may want to wait until the next commercial, then until the show is over, and maybe until tomorrow. They will try to keep pushing it off. We do the same thing as adults with some of our responsibilities, maybe lawn mowing.

CHOICES

You come home from work and know you should mow the lawn, but you're tired, so you'll wait until after you eat dinner. Maybe I'll wait until the weekend. Then Saturday comes, and you decide to wait until after lunch or something like that. That's an example of myself, but we all do something like this in some way.

Responsibility is a thing one is required to do as part of a job, role, or legal obligation. As a child, you have responsibilities to help prepare you for when you're older. They help you get used to having to do things. But as a child, the choices you make won't affect the rest of your life. There may be consequences at that moment, but soon after that, it won't make any difference. You are still innocent or blameless. But there's a point in our life when the choices we make will affect the rest of our life. What that means is, we are responsible for the choices we make. That means we are no longer innocent and we decide to make that choice. Now we will have consequences of some sort for every choice we make.

There is an age when this happens, but it's different for everyone. I believe it's somewhere between eleven and thirteen, but that is only an opinion, not a fact. Look back on your past and think of something you did or said that still affects your life. Not something someone did to you but a choice you made. Something you are responsible for and guilty of. Think about that and the age you were when it happened. Also, Jewish people celebrate the bar and bat mitzvah at twelve or thirteen. That marks when a Jewish boy (bar) or girl (bat) becomes an adult. As an adult, you are responsible for everything you do and say.

LIFE

As you age, you learn how to take care of yourself. You learn how to do all those things that others have done for you. You can also start to do what you want to do. But you have to learn how to do everything. Someone has to teach you how to do everything except what you want to do. You already have something inside of you that tells you what you want to do, but you have to learn the things you need to do. For example, as a child, you might have wanted to put that toy in your mouth. An older person has to teach you that you don't need that toy in your mouth. When you are a child, someone is always in control, and you have to listen to them. You can say no and refuse to do things, but your choices are limited. As you age, your choices become more often, more important, and more your choice.

I'm guessing everyone can agree that our teenage years are the craziest, most confusing, and most trying years of our lives. Please don't get me wrong. Life is always challenging. But during our teenage years, nothing makes any sense. At the same time, we feel like we know everything and have it under control. We usually hide what's happening in our lives from our parents and every other authority figure. If we decide to open up, it's only to a certain point, and half of it's a lie. We feel like we know what we're doing. Older people have no idea what it's like to go through what we're going through. The world has completely changed since they were this age.

We pretend to listen to older people. But we believe that our friends, who are the same age as us, know more about life than

CHOICES

older people. We listen to them. In our teenage years, and usually throughout our twenties, we genuinely believe our friends know more about life than our parents or any older people. Those our own age, doing the same things we are doing, are the people we get advice from and actually listen to. But older people, anyone ten years or more older than us, have no idea what they are talking about. Maybe that crazy uncle who got into a bunch of trouble might know some things but not those boring parents. Regardless of the advice we get, whom it's from or whom we listen to or follow, as a teenager the choices we make are our choices, and we are responsible for them.

In a perfect world, your parents, your father and mother, would teach you all about life. First, they would teach you the things you need to know to be able to take care of yourself. You would start to learn those things when you're about two years old. You would learn things like walking, talking, and using the bathroom. And that never stops. Throughout your life, you're learning something new that helps you to take care of yourself, and you always need someone to teach you how to do it.

First, you learn how to eat (eventually the best foods to eat), how to exercise, the best way to relax, and possibly, down the road, the best walker to use. We are always learning, and we always need someone to help us. In a perfect world, your parents would also be the perfect example. They would have all the perfect words and actions for you to follow. Healthy habits, proper language, treating others kindly, and just living a good life. If you would experience

LIFE

that and could learn from them, then you would have a solid foundation of values and rules. Then in your teenage years, when you would start to become independent and make your own choices, you would have that solid foundation and be willing to listen to and follow your parents' instructions. Then your teen years would give you the experience you need to live your own life. So by the time you turn twenty, you will be ready to find a spouse and start a family. And the whole circle would start over again. You would do for your children what your parents did for you.

We do not live in a perfect world. Not even one of us is perfect. How do you learn how to live a perfect life from other people who don't know how to live a perfect life? We can receive valuable advice from people who have gone through what we are experiencing, which is very helpful. But the instructions and advice we receive from our parents or the people who raised us are the best advice and instructions we can get. If not our parents or the people who raised us, there's always an older person in our life who has good advice. That advice and those instructions are what we need to hear, not what we want to hear.

Sadly, we don't realize how valuable that advice is until we are around thirty. That's when we say, "Oh no, they were right." Thirty years old is about the time you finally realize those friends you've been listening to your whole life have no idea what they are talking about, and neither do you. You understand that people older than you have experienced these things and know what is needed to get through them. People your own age may know as much as you,

CHOICES

but that's about it. Now all those things that older people have told you while growing up start to make sense, and you begin to follow them. That makes you realize life isn't going quite the way it should be. What do you do now?

If life isn't going the way you hoped it would be, this is the point when you realize things need to change. How things need to change is different for everyone. By the time you're thirty, a lot has happened in your life. Maybe you have gone to college, have a career, are raising a family, or none of those things. Maybe you can't keep a job, maybe you've had three kids with three different people, maybe you're alone and have never had kids, or maybe none of these things happened. Wherever you are in life, when you turn thirty, you have a feeling that something needs to change. You may know what needs to change, or you may not. But you have a feeling inside of you that something needs to be different than it is.

By the time you turn forty, if things haven't changed or aren't going the way you expected them to be going, you may fall apart. That is commonly known as a midlife crisis. You have had an expectation of how your life would be going, but none of that is happening. You are constantly thinking about one particular thing. You feel like if this one thing happens in your life, everything else will fall into place and you'll be fine. I call this living in the future. You've been waiting for that one particular thing to happen and then everything else will fall into place. You may have been waiting for it to happen since high school.

I've played music most of my life, and I wanted to become a rock star. I thought my whole life and everything in it would fall

LIFE

into place as soon as I became a rock star. I'd have more money and could quit my job. That'd be perfect. But that never happened, and honestly, with the life I was living then, it's for the better. We need to live for what is happening right here, right now, today. It's easy to live in the future, thinking about what you want to have happen, or in the past, thinking about how different things would be if that and that would or wouldn't have happened. But if you do that, you miss out on everything that is happening now. You need to plan for the future but live for today.

If you're in a meeting staring at the clock, waiting for it to be over, you will miss everything being talked about while you think about what you're going to eat when you get out of it. That's what happens in our lives when we live in the future. We are constantly thinking about and waiting for that one thing to happen. Then we miss out on everything that is happening. I've heard from many people that their kids grew up so fast. If you only focus on that one thing happening, you will either miss out on your kids growing up or on your own life. The same thing happens when you focus on your mistakes. We all make mistakes. If not daily, very close to it. If you only focus on your past mistakes, you will miss out on life. Learn from your mistakes, and they will help you in the future.

You are not perfect, and you will make mistakes; learn from them. If you were learning how to ride a bike, fell off, and never tried to ride it again, you would think you're bad at riding a bike. You would feel like other people can do it but you're not good at it. If you tried to ride a bunch of times and fell off every time, then you would know that riding a bike isn't for you. But if you tried a few times and it worked out, now you can keep learning more about it to make it easier. That's life. Do you give up, or do you try again? Do you learn from what you did wrong or focus on how bad you are? Wouldn't it be easier if you had someone there to hold on to the bike while you learned how to pedal and steer?

This life makes no sense. It's very confusing, and we have no idea what we are doing or how to get through it. Some instructions would definitely be nice. We all need some help, but that is the hardest thing to admit or ask for. If you want something in your life to change, things to be different, simply ask for help. Some humans can help a little, but ask God for help, and things will start to change. God will keep your bike steady while you learn how to pedal and steer.

How and Why

How am I responsible for my choices? I have everyone telling me what I should do, how I should do it, when I should do it, and why I should do it. Someone is trying to tell me how to live my life everywhere I go. I know I make some choices, but I usually follow what everyone else says is the right thing to do. How can I be guilty of my choices when I barely know what I'm doing? If I had someone keeping the bike steady while I learned how to pedal and steer, I might take some responsibility for my choices. But while I'm learning on my own, all alone, there's no reason to blame me and call me guilty. I'm just trying to figure out what the best way to live is for me while I have everyone else trying to tell me how to do it.

Where do our decisions come from? What influences us so much that we give in to it and follow that choice? We do things every day that we don't think about. We just do them. We call this our daily routine. I like to wake up, have breakfast, have coffee, brush my teeth, shower, and take on the day. Over the weekend, things may

CHOICES

change a little here and there, but it stays pretty close to the same routine. When there is a significant change to my routine, it throws my whole day out of whack. My routine is what I'm comfortable with, and it's how it needs to be. It is a big deal for all of us when a significant change happens—like moving to a new city, starting a completely different career, having a baby, or eating a new cereal. If you are used to eating something like Froot Loops every morning and suddenly have oatmeal, that can be scary. Whether big or small, change can be difficult.

How do we begin a routine? What choices do we repeatedly make to get comfortable with certain things? What influences us to make these choices, and where do these choices come from inside of us? Our choices come from our conscious and subconscious minds. The choices we make are called our will. Our will is the power to control our actions and emotions. It is what we choose to do and say. We have the ability and freedom to do, say, and feel whatever we want to. But there are consequences that go along with every single choice we make. If you make a good choice, the consequences are good. Just like a bad choice has bad consequences, right? No, not at all. The consequences of our choices teach us things. We need to learn how to control our thoughts, words, emotions, and actions. And that's easy, a piece of cake. No, not at all.

We are literally slaves to our thoughts, emotions, words, and actions. We need to develop self-control. Then we can control ourselves and our choices. To develop self-control, we need to understand what influences our choices and how those things influence

HOW AND WHY

our choices. First, as I mentioned before, our subconscious mind influences our conscious mind, and our conscious mind processes all our choices. Your subconscious mind stores away every experience you ever had, but you're lucky if you can remember last week. Those experiences shape your attitudes and beliefs. Also, they affect your feelings and emotions. Our memories, feelings, and emotions develop what we like, dislike, and hate. Combining your attitude, beliefs, feelings, and memories about something can help you make a fairly decent decision.

Suppose you jumped off a staircase as a child. That helps you develop your knowledge of gravity. You probably didn't know the word *gravity*, but you learned if you jump off a step, you land on the floor. That's how gravity works. If you jump off something, you won't float away. You'll hit the ground. So you jump off the first step of the staircase, and it's fun. Now you want to keep going higher. You move up to the second step, jump, then the third step, and keep repeating that. Eventually, you get to a step from which you jump off that hurts when you land. Now you know not to go any higher. You still want to go higher but don't want to get hurt. That becomes what you look forward to because of how fun jumping off that step is. You still have that want, that urge, or desire to go higher, but you don't want to get hurt. Then your neighbor gets a trampoline, which is much more exciting, and you can go so much higher and not get hurt.

That's how your subconscious can get shaped by something as simple as jumping off a step. Your belief would be that jumping from

CHOICES

something too high will hurt. Your attitude would be that you like to jump off things, and you want to go as high as you can without getting hurt. Your feeling would be pleasure, your emotion would be happy. You would remember all those things and know how high the highest step you jumped off was. Now when the choice comes up to jump off something again, you will have thoughts about it and reason it out before you make a choice. That is how our subconscious mind influences our conscious mind.

You gained knowledge about jumping off a step and jumping on a trampoline, and they were both a lot of fun. But now you know you will hurt yourself if you go too high without a soft landing, so you are careful about your actions. Then a friend says, "I bet you could jump off that garage roof and not get hurt." That is when your subconscious mind begins to influence your conscious mind. Now you can start to think about what they said and reason it out. Understand that your subconscious doesn't make any decisions. It gives you the information you have gained throughout life. It influences or helps your conscious mind, and your conscious mind helps you make a decision. You know why you shouldn't jump off that garage, but you still really want to. You know that roof is higher than the highest step you jumped off. You know how much that step hurt, and you can only imagine how much it would hurt jumping from the height of that garage roof. You also know how much fun it is to jump off things. That is reasoning. You are explaining to yourself why you should or shouldn't do something. Having thoughts and reasoning are what our conscious mind does. Our subconscious mind influences our thoughts and reasoning.

HOW AND WHY

Your friend asks you to jump off the garage roof then you weigh your options. You tell your friend, "I know if I jump from something that high, I'll get hurt, the ground is hard." Immediately your friend says, "We can get a mattress from my bedroom and put it where you will land." Again, you have to think about what they said, reason it out, and make a decision. Then you say, "Okay, we can try that." After that you learn some valuable lessons. But that, right there, is life.

You are making choices, learning the good and bad in each choice, and applying it to the next choice. The problem we face is we are constantly making a choice, and if our conscious or subconscious mind changes for a split second, so will our choices. For example, many of us try to eat healthy foods. We usually plan out what we are going to eat for the week. But then you smell that unhealthy food, and your plans fall apart.

Now we need to understand what influences our subconscious. Where do our memories come from? How do we have experiences? Our five senses allow us to experience things. Our five senses are seeing, hearing, smelling, tasting, and touching. They help you have a complete experience. Think about when you are enjoying your favorite food. First, you see it, then you smell it, maybe touch it, possibly hear it sizzling, and finally taste it. Each of those things stays in your subconscious, and you know how to respond the next time you have this meal. And this is where self-control is needed. We know the good and bad parts of the things we want. We know an ice cream sundae with tons of toppings would taste great. We also know that it has a lot of sugar, and that's not good. We all have different tastes in food, and these are just examples, but we all have choices to make. We need self-control to keep us from doing things we know are bad for us. Do we listen to the knowledge we've gained through our experiences, or do we listen to our urges, wants, and desires?

Our surroundings are a significant influence on us. Where you grow up, how you grow up, and the people you are around while growing up are your biggest influences. Each one of these things influences your perspective. If you grow up in the middle of a city with a lot of people and buildings and then move to a small town, that would be a huge change. The same thing is true the other way around, going from a small town to a big city. But moving an hour down the road can be a huge change. You might know one or two people if you're lucky, but it is all new. You might have been there a few times, but living there is completely different. Think about how the environment you grew up in shaped the way you receive information from your five senses. Whatever setting you grew up in is what you are used to being around.

That is how our opinions begin to get shaped. We know how things were where we grew up and when we grew up. We know the beliefs our parents, siblings, relatives, friends, and other people gave us. Also, the music we listen to, the social media we're part of, and the TV shows we watch, all affect our beliefs. For example, when I was growing up, I had things I promised myself I would never do. But if I didn't do them by the time I was sixteen, I started to do them at that age.

HOW AND WHY

I promised myself I would never start smoking. When I was very young, my dad died from lung cancer, and I felt like smoking was utterly evil. I had my first alcoholic drink at sixteen, and a cigarette followed it. Obviously, at that age, I wasn't smoking a lot, but my smoking and drinking habits got worse as I aged. Then other bad habits entered the picture as well. I started playing music when I was thirteen years old. By the time I was sixteen, I wanted to be a rock star. I never got far as a musician, but I still tried to live like the musicians I admired—or at least how I thought they lived. I hoped to make enough money playing music to quit my job. Then I could drink all day and play music all night. Whatever we are around, whatever surrounds us, will develop our beliefs, change our beliefs, or form new beliefs in us. Those beliefs come from what we see and hear. That is two of our five senses influencing us. Our choice is, do we stay in this environment, or do we leave?

I got stuck in a life that was going absolutely nowhere. I had a bad drinking problem, and that led to other bad habits and choices. I know what it's like to hate your life. You hate everything you do and want to change, but you don't know how because this is the only life you've ever had and the only one you know how to live. I ended up in that life because it was a lot of fun at first. You're hanging out with friends and having some good times. But somewhere deep inside yourself, you know what you're doing is wrong. It's a bad choice. But instead of choosing to stop doing what you're already doing, you start doing something else to cover up your feelings about the other thing you're doing. That is how and why

CHOICES

we start doing more of one thing and then get into all kinds of other things. If you turn off your conscious mind, you don't have to think about what you are doing or weigh your options. You cover your thoughts and reasoning with more bad ideas.

We all do this in some way; not all of us have a drinking or a drug problem, but every one of us makes bad decisions. Bad decisions negatively affect your life. Think of life as a math problem. If you add a bad decision with a negative outcome, there are many things that can equal. Most likely, it will equal regret; hopefully, it equals "and they lived happily ever after," but the chances of that are slim. Bad decisions have a negative outcome, but we are able to choose how they will affect us. What do I mean by that?

When you go through tough times, how do you respond to them? Do you blame other people for what they have done? Do you feel like if someone hadn't given you that unhealthy food, you wouldn't have had to eat it? Do you try to handle the situation the best you can? Do you try to stay strong and positive regardless of what you are going through? Do you cover up the way you feel with another bad idea? If you jump off the garage roof onto a mattress and sprain your ankle, do you change how you walk and hope no one will notice? Do you suddenly have a cool strut you never had before? If you break a lamp in the house, do you try to glue it back together? We can do many more things, but admitting you made a mistake is the best choice. Then look back on what affected and influenced your choice and what you could do differently in the future. In other words, learn from your mistakes. Stop regretting what you've already done, start to learn from it, and begin to live a better life.

One of our biggest problems is that we use dirt to try to clean ourselves off. If you got a mark on your hand from a black permanent marker, would you use another black permanent marker to try to erase that mark? Hopefully not. But when we are in a bad mood, and things aren't going right, we usually listen to music that fits that mood. Then we feel worse and even angrier. When we are down and feeling negative, we need something to pick us up and help us feel and think positively.

Going to your local bar or club may give you people to be around and help you take your mind off things, but it doesn't change anything, or if it does change things, it will probably make them worse. The same happens if you go to close friends and they tell you how wrong you are and how much you need to change your life. Negative influences create negative attitudes. Negative attitudes create negative beliefs. Negative beliefs give you a negative outlook on yourself and everything around you. Your attitudes and beliefs are part of your subconscious mind. When you have negativity in your subconscious mind, that influences your conscious mind. Then most of your thoughts and reasoning become negative. Then it becomes easy to do things that harm you physically and emotionally. You no longer value your own life. Also, when weighing your options and reasoning, the negative thoughts outnumber or outweigh the positive ones. Then it becomes much easier to do things you know are harmful to yourself and those around you. Negativity is everywhere and constantly influences us.

CHOICES

The biggest question we can ask is, how do we eliminate all these negative thoughts? How do we start to have positive feelings and thoughts? What we need is something that will affect us from the inside out. Instead of coming in through our five senses, it affects our perspective, and we can perceive things in a new way. It's the same idea as someone holding the handlebars and the back of the seat on a bike as we learn how to pedal. This life is a challenge. We grow up with all kinds of beliefs and attitudes. We learn different things from different people, and things change as we age. None of us has all the answers. We don't know it all and never will. How can we get through this crazy, insane, misleading thing called life?

There is only one answer, and his name is Jesus Christ. All you need to do is allow him to hold on to your bike. He'll keep it steady. The only thing you need to do is steer.

React and Respond

Our most significant influence in this life is our surroundings. What we focus on the most is what we concentrate on the most. If you want to grow a garden and know nothing about it, you have to learn how to do it. Now you are focused on growing a garden and concentrating on how to do it. We often focus on negative things but don't realize it. For example, if you watch TV with a lot of violence, play video games with a lot of violence, hear songs with a lot of violence, and experience violence in your life, you focus on violence. Then it becomes a normal part of life. The things that you're around most often become normal, especially the things that affect all your five senses. Seeing and hearing something often will make it a normal part of your life. But it becomes second nature if you experience it with all your senses. For example, if you start to drive a car, you experience that with all your senses. You might have walked or ridden a bike before that, but it only takes a short time until driving a car becomes second nature. You see the open road and all the other vehicles, hear your favorite music or

CHOICES

silence, grip the steering wheel, smell your car, and usually have some food or drink with you. It almost becomes a part of you. Then when you smell that certain smell, it reminds you of your car. That is your subconscious at work. A certain smell reminds you of something, bringing up feelings, emotions, attitudes, and beliefs. It takes you back to certain moments of your life. How you respond to that is your choice. You can react or respond.

What does it mean to react? When you react to something, you are doing it without thinking. It just happens. When you respond to something, you are using your conscious mind. You think about it and reason it out. Then you can give a self-controlled, thought-out response. You think about something and determine the best response to whatever happens to you. If someone jumped out from the other side of a wall and scared you, you would probably jump first, which is a reaction. Then you decide how to respond. If your surroundings are mostly violent, you hit the person without thinking twice about it. But another option is to tell the person, "Never do that again." That would be a thought-out, self-controlled response.

Understand that children react to things. Whatever happens to a child, they only have the ability to react to it. As an adult, we have the ability to respond to it. A child likes something because it is pleasing to one of their five senses. Also, they don't like something because it isn't pleasing to one of their five senses. A child can pick a favorite color by looking at colors. They look at them, and one looks better than the rest, and they say, "That's my favorite color."

REACT AND RESPOND

An adult can barely choose a favorite color because they reason it out. They like this color when they're in this mood, and that color during this season and a different shade may look nicer. If a child is playing with a toy and you take it from them, they will get upset. Every child reacts differently, but they will be angry. If you give a child a toy, they will play with it. Maybe for only a second or two, but they will play with it.

With an adult, you have no idea how they will respond. Think about it. If you give a toy to an adult, they could say, "Thank you," then grab and play with it. Or they could say, "What? You think I act like a child, so you're giving me a toy to play with? You don't know me." And a thousand other responses. Children react to whatever is happening. They don't have the ability to think about something. They can't figure it out. That's why they need to be taught and disciplined. They don't know or understand right and wrong. They only know what they like and what they want. If they are not taught and shown things as a child, they won't have a foundation to learn from as they grow older. And if you don't have any authority figure to listen to as a child, you won't listen to any authority figures as you age.

Children don't know or understand what right and wrong are. They only know that someone older got upset, and they don't want to upset them. The more we learn as a child, the more of a foundation we will have for the rest of our life. We are going to get in trouble, do stupid things, and make a lot of mistakes. That's part of life. But when fundamental values are taught to us when we are

CHOICES

young, our troubles won't be as bad as we age. Also, a child learns by watching. If you tell a child to do one thing but you do something else, they will do what they see. Children look up to adults, especially their parents or whoever is raising them. They will become a miniature version of you. But as soon as they have the ability to choose, they will try to become their own person. But a boy is his father, and a girl is her mother. As long as a child has had a relationship with their parents as they age, they will be just like their parents. They will go through some years of rebellion, but they can't escape who they are.

"That's why it's not my fault." Do you say that and blame others? Some things happen to us that aren't our fault, and there's nothing we can do about that. But how often do you blame someone else for a choice you made? How often do you think that that wouldn't have happened if they hadn't given you that option? It sounds stupid like that, but we do it all the time. I know all about it. I used to think, "If the alcohol hadn't been there, I wouldn't have drunk it, and then all that other stuff wouldn't have happened." If I didn't have the option to drink, I wouldn't have, but since it was there, I decided to.

We are all responsible for the choices we make. Every single decision we make is our responsibility. We have a lot of help to make one decision, between our conscious and subconscious minds, our five senses, our surroundings, every other experience we've had, and our knowledge. But we still can't make the right choice. Or at least I can't. If your life is going perfectly, you have peace of mind, no stress, no anxiety, and you get a great night's sleep every night, then you're doing good. If not, then you need some more help. It would help if you had someone to hold on to your bicycle while you learn how to pedal.

What would it be like to be an adult without any stress, worry, or anxiety? Imagine having the knowledge of an adult but the innocence of a child. You wouldn't be concerned at all about how others looked at you. Even if you were naked, it wouldn't bother you. You would be like a small child running around without their diaper on. You would know who you are and who you need to be. What I mean by that is you would know exactly what your purpose in life is and who you need to be to accomplish that purpose.

Take it one step further, and imagine you would have no evil intentions. You would have no evil thoughts, words, or actions. If every one of us were like that, we wouldn't have any problems with each other. That is God's original design of human beings. The first story in the Bible is about the creation of everything and the first two human beings, Adam and Eve. Their minds would have been just like this. They didn't have the knowledge of good and evil. The only thing they knew was love. They knew who they were, needed to be, and what they needed to do. Or, to put it another way, they had meaning, purpose, and love. God created the Garden of Eden to put Adam and Eve into it, and their job was to take care of it. Their purpose was to care for the Garden of Eden and be loved by God. God took care of all their needs. God planted all kinds of trees and plants for them to eat from. At that point, there weren't any thorns or thistles, and the land was easier to take care of.

CHOICES

The Tree of the Knowledge of Good and Evil was in the middle of the garden. God told both Adam and Eve not to eat from the Tree of the Knowledge of Good and Evil because, on that day, they would die. They could eat from any other tree in the garden. Then Satan came into the garden as a snake. First, he took Adam and Eve's focus off God. Satan got their attention. Then he questioned what God said.

He asked Eve, "Didn't God say that you can eat from any tree in the garden?" (Gen 3:1b-5, NIV)

Eve told Satan, "We may eat from any tree in the garden, but from the Tree of the Knowledge of Good and Evil, God said do not eat from it, do not touch it or you will die."

Then Satan said, "You will not die. God knows that when you eat from it, your eyes will be opened, and you will become like him, knowing both good and evil."

That sounded good to Eve, so she ate fruit from the tree. Adam was there with her. She gave him the fruit, and then he ate it too.

The knowledge they gained from the fruit opened their eyes, and they knew they were naked. As soon as they ate from the tree, they became self-aware. They became aware of themselves and felt shame. As soon as they felt shame, they wanted to hide it. They sewed fig leaves together to cover themselves. Then they heard God walking through the garden, and they hid from him. They knew what they did was wrong—or in other words, they knew they were guilty. Can you imagine that, in the blink of an eye going from the innocence of a child—only knowing love, never feeling anything negative—to feeling complete shame, guilt, and regret?

REACT AND RESPOND

Guilt is knowing you did something wrong. It isn't a feeling. It's knowledge. God gave us guilt so that we know we are doing something wrong. And usually, we do our best to hide everything we do wrong, which is exactly what Adam and Eve did. They hid from God when they heard him walking in the garden.

God called out to Adam and asked him, "Where are you?" (Gen 3:9, NIV)

To this day, this is what God does to every one of us. God knows exactly where we are, but if we answer him, we acknowledge him, and that's what God wants. God wants us to acknowledge him and turn back to him. Adam and Eve knew God; they lived with him, but Satan turned them away from God. Satan wasn't trying to get Adam and Eve to follow him. He just wanted to take their attention away from God, and it's still the same for us today. We turn our backs toward God and can't pay attention to him. He listens, helps, and loves us, but we don't know him.

God is calling out your name, but it's your choice to answer him. Do you say, "Here I am!" or do you keep hiding and pretend everything will be okay?

When God called out to Adam, Adam said, "I heard you walking in the garden, and I was afraid because I was naked, so I hid." (Gen 3:10-11a, NIV)

God asks him, "Who told you that you were naked?" God knew Adam gained shame from eating the fruit, but God wanted Adam and us to know that shame wasn't from him.

The shame is from Satan. Satan wants us to feel bad about ourselves. He wants us to hate ourselves and everything we do.

CHOICES

The worse we feel about ourselves, the easier it is to tempt us into doing all kinds of things. And we feel lost. When we hate ourselves, we need something to help us have a new direction, and Satan will tempt us with all sorts of things. God allows us to feel shame so we will turn to him and ask for help. If we didn't need help, we would never turn to God.

Right after God asked Adam, "Who told you were naked?" he asked, "Did you eat from the tree I commanded you not to eat from?" (Gen 3:11b-13, NIV)

Adam said, "The woman, who you gave to me, she gave me the fruit, and I ate." Right away Adam blamed both God and Eve.

God asked Eve, "What have you done?"

Eve said, "The serpent tricked me, and I ate."

That was the truth. Satan did trick Eve. What Satan said sounded good to her, so she ate. Understand that the only thing Adam and Eve didn't have in the Garden of Eden was the full wisdom of God. They had some wisdom, but not all of it. They couldn't have all of it because that's more than the human brain can handle. We can't have all of it today either, but we still keep trying. Adam was standing there watching and listening to everything that was happening. He saw Eve eat the fruit, and he still chose to eat it. That's why it is said that Adam committed the first sin. He intentionally sinned.

After God talked to Eve, he told the serpent, "Because you have done this, cursed are you above all livestock and wild animals. You will crawl on your belly and eat dust for the rest of your days. I will put hostility between you and the woman and between her offspring, he will strike your head, and you will strike his heel." (Gen 3:14-15, NIV)

The last line is a reference to Jesus Christ. Jesus crushed Satan, and Satan nipped at his heel. From the beginning, God had a plan to redeem all of humanity. God has given us the ability to choose him. Do we choose him?

Then God turned to Eve and said, "I will greatly increase your labor pains, with pain, you will give birth to children. Your desire will be for your husband, and he will rule over you." (Gen 3:16, NIV)

Men and women are equal. Both of their opinions and thoughts matter. But the man usually has the final say. For example, there can be a lot of arguments and discussions about a vacation. But when Dad finally says, "Okay, let's do that," you go on vacation. Because men and women can't always agree, a lot of strain is put on a marriage. Everyone wants control, and it's hard to listen to someone else. Marriage and childbirth bring a lot of joy, but pain also comes from both.

God tells Adam, "Because you have listened to your wife and ate from the tree I commanded you not to eat from, cursed is the ground. Because of you, in painful toil, you will eat of it all the days of your life. It will produce thorns and thistles, but you will eat the grain of the field. By the sweat of your brow, you will eat food until you return to the ground, for out of it you were taken, for you are dust, and to dust, you will return." (Gen 3:17-19, NIV)

God would've given them everything they needed, but now they had to learn to care for themselves. After that God made

CHOICES

garments of skin from an animal for Adam and Eve. Even though Adam and Eve did exactly what God told them not to do, he still covered their shame, their nakedness. Then God kicked them out of the garden.

That is where we are to this very day. We are born separated from God. We can't see Satan or any of his demons, and we can't see God or any of his angels because we are separated from all of it. We can't see any of it, but it is all around us, and we are affected by what happens. This might sound crazy, but look at your life, how messed up it is, how lost you feel, and how easy it is to see Jesus Christ as a joke. Satan does everything he can to make Christianity look and sound ridiculous.

God kicked Adam and Eve out of the Garden of Eden, and they lost all the power God had given them. They had a purpose in the garden, and that gave them knowledge of their true identity. They knew who they were and who they needed to be to accomplish their purpose. They also had meaning, which was to live in the garden, take care of it, and enjoy life. They had real love—love for and from God, love for themselves and each other. That was all lost when they sinned. That is why figuring out who we are and what we should do with our lives is so hard. They still had life. Blood ran through their veins, but that's about it. Now they lived in a world filled with evil. That's exactly where we are now, living in a world filled with evil. It's inside of us and all around us.

We have a choice to make. Do we follow this world and its ways, or do we follow God and his ways? We are living in a world that is between heaven and hell. Do we follow this world and end up in hell or follow God and end up in heaven? We are all born with evil intentions already inside of us. God told Adam and Eve in the garden to "be fruitful and multiply." The knowledge of good and evil spreads to the next generation through sex. God knew that evil and sin would spread, and he allowed it to happen. God gave us free will.

Free will is the ability to make whatever choice we want to. God cannot control our choices or actions, and neither can anyone else. God allowed evil to spread to all humanity so that we would have the ability to choose to love him and not do it naturally. If we didn't need help, we would never turn to God. That is all of humanity. We all lost purpose, meaning, and love. We live in between two worlds simultaneously: one we see and the other is unseen. Every one of us has evil inside of us that causes us to sin, to go against God's commandments.

There is a point in our lives when wrong choices seem to take over. It feels like wrong choices cover our lives and like our only ability is to do what is wrong. For most of us, if not all of us, this happens in our teens. We have an inner urge to do what we know as "the right thing," but we continue to do the wrong thing. And the more wrong choices you make, the easier it becomes. It begins to seem normal and okay. These choices have something to do with control, which is power. We also want money and sex. It looks like this: doing what you want, to get what you want, when you want it. Sex is a natural part of life, but like most things we like, we want more as soon as we get a little. Because of our choices, we might gain physical issues like illnesses, disabilities, being harmed, or something else. These things could separate us from the people who care about us. But when we know we are doing things that we shouldn't be doing, we physically separate ourselves from the people who could help us, the people who love us.

That's the point when life is about to fall apart. You worry about everything, especially your future. What's going to happen next? Now you are drowning in stress, anxiety, and unrest. Then something happens in your life that destroys any hope you have left. That's when life becomes dark. Nothing matters. You hate everything, including yourself and everything you do. You have no hope, joy, or reason to keep trying and are ready to give up.

These are the steps we go through in this life. Hopefully, you've only experienced some of this and not all of it. When you get to that point where nothing matters, you have two choices: get help or die. Please get help. I know all about it because I've been there. I was very close to giving up on life. I didn't look for help, but it came to me, and I'm so thankful it did. These are the steps we go through.

- **Step 1:** the evil that's inside of you takes over. It gains control.

- **Step 2:** the most common types of evil—sex, money, and power—become a significant part of your life. Understand that we want power because it gives us more control. Power equals control.

- **Step 3:** you might gain physical problems like illnesses and diseases or become handicapped or maybe not. But somehow you will separate yourself from those who love and care about you.

- **Step 4:** something will happen in your life that will cause a lot of anxiety, stress, and unrest.

- **Step 5:** you continue to do things that hurt yourself and others. Things continue to happen that destroy whatever hope you have left.

- **Step 6:** you have no hope, joy, or peace. In other words, nothing matters. Life feels like darkness, and you are ready to give up.

- **Step 7:** is the last step, and that is death.

We all go through this at some point in our lives. How many of these steps we take depends on when we turn to God. That is the most important choice we must make while we're alive. We can only turn toward God through faith in Jesus Christ. The real question is, do you want a better life with peace, hope, and joy? The only thing God wants from you is your love and trust. But you can't love or trust anyone if you don't know them. We need to learn who God is and how he does things. From my own experiences, I know how easy it is to brush all this God stuff off to the side. I felt like every god people talked about was something someone made up to help explain how the world worked. We have technology and science that can explain these things. We no longer need gods. But then I got to know God when I was very close to ending my own life, and everything changed after that. Give God a chance, get to know him, and see what happens.

The big question is, why did God put the Tree of Knowledge in the garden? God knows everything, everything that has and will happen. He is everywhere and is in complete control. So why would God allow any of this to happen? When God created us, he gave us free will. That is the ability to do whatever you want to, choose whatever you want, and live however you want. God wants us to choose to love him, not naturally do it. The knowledge of good and evil separated us from God, and now we have to choose to love him. We will only choose to love him if we need help. We wouldn't need help if we didn't have problems. We need to understand that when we are separated and turned away from God, many other gods can enter our lives, and those are the gods that we have to please.

Every urge we have that becomes more important to us than God becomes a god. Now we have to do what that urge wants us to, or we get distraught. For example, alcohol was more important to me than anything else. When I tried to drink one beer, it turned into five or six. I didn't control it, and I needed to fill that urge or please that god. If there is anything in your life that has more control over you than you do over it, that is a god. When you turn back to God,

REACT AND RESPOND

he will begin to remove those urges, and that is when you start to have peace in your life. Otherwise, you are a slave to that urge. We all have urges that negatively affect us, and God will remove them if we ask him to. Simply put, God wants us to choose to love him, and he will change us from the inside, and then we will have reasons to love him. That's when life will become better.

God

The next question is, who is God, and why should any one of us ask him for help? People say he has unconditional love. But I see God kills people and makes them suffer. Also, I'm living life, and I know how hard it is. I don't see this so-called unconditional love. When I buy a new appliance, it comes with an instruction manual. What does this life come with? Doubt, confusion, anxiety, grief, and a whole list of other painful things. What's the point of any of this?

Who is God? God is the one who put us here, who gave us life. I've heard it called "the gift of life." Most of us do not consider life to be a gift. A hand grenade wrapped up really nicely, but not a gift. God created the whole universe and everything in it. He created all of us and everything we can see—and another world we can't see. Everything God created has either lasted since he created it or can reproduce itself. Plants drop seeds and grow again. Animals and humans have males and females who come together and make a baby. When two opposite sexes come together, they can form a baby. Humans do not create anything. We invent, build, and make a lot of things. But the materials we use to build and make things come from God's original creation. When humans make or build something, it has to be remade or rebuilt over and over again and again. Again, we cannot create things. We can only use the things that God created to make different and new things.

The big question is, why did God put us here? The bigger question is, why did God put you here? There are many different answers to that question, but the root of it is that he loves you. The only thing that he wants from you is for you to love him. So it's very simple. A God whom we can't see, who gave us a life that makes no sense, who allows us to go through all this pain and suffering while we keep making mistakes that make life harder, wants us to love him. And if my dad beat me senseless while I was growing up, left for thirty years, and then came back and said, "I love you," I'm sure I'd say, "I love you too." Then we'd hug and live happily ever after. Of course not. None of us would respond that way. So why does God expect us to love him after this life has beat us up and left us for dead? To be honest, he doesn't. God doesn't expect you to turn to him and say, "I love you, God. Thanks for letting me suffer. It's been great." God truly wants you to turn to him and ask for help. Every single one of us needs help.

Help is one of the hardest things for us to ask for. It's easy to ask for things. You might need some money, maybe a ride, or some food. But to admit you are wrong, make mistakes, and need help is extremely challenging. Usually, at some point, we realize we are wrong. We aren't living a good life, and we are making a lot of bad choices. We will notice that in our lives, but admitting it to ourselves is not easy, and even thinking about admitting it to someone else is insane. We acknowledge we are weak when we admit we are wrong and need help, and we all want to be strong. That might be physically, emotionally, mentally, socially, or some other way, but we all want others to see us as strong in some way. And throughout our whole life, we are taught we need to be strong. Climb any mountain; overcome every obstacle; try, try again; and never give up. The harder you try, the more you will succeed. We've heard these things our whole lives. We are also taught that there's no reason to ask for help. People tell us things like, "You can do it." And if you ask someone for help, you have to trust that person, which is another challenge. When you trust someone, most of the time, they will let you down. It's hard to trust other people. We already know what we ourselves are capable of, and then we see what other people are doing. Trust is something that people have to earn. We don't just give it to them. People have to prove they are trustworthy. It's hard to ask for help when you don't trust anyone.

In the Bible, Psalms 139:13 says, "Indeed you created my inner parts, you wove me in my mother's womb." Luke 12:7 says, "Even the hairs on my head you have numbered." (Version LEB, Lexington English Bible)

There are many other verses to go with these, but I want to get to the main point. God knew you before you were born, and he knows everything about you, even the number of hairs on your

CHOICES

head. God knows you in a very intimate way. But if God knows everything about us, he should know that we need help and how we need help. Why doesn't God help us? Why doesn't he snap his fingers and make it all better? One reason is that God wants us to acknowledge him. When we ask him for help, we admit to ourselves that he is truly there. He is real. We don't need to know everything about him. We only need to acknowledge him by asking for help.

Asking God for help is praying. Praying is to address a request or an expression of thanks to God. Prayer, quite simply, is talking to God. (Source: Oxford languages)

Think about that. You can go to God, the Creator of the entire universe, and speak directly to him. It doesn't matter who you are, where you are, your condition, or how well you know him. He will hear you. God wants nothing more than to hear from you. Your condition depends on how rough life has been for you. Think of yourself as a tire. The more miles you put on a tire, the less tread it has. As a tire loses its tread, it loses its traction, can't keep the car on the road, and can't do its job. If life wears you down and you can't do your job, you can't live, but God still loves you. But living is tough when you don't know your purpose and meaning.

One of the gifts that God gave us as humans is free will. What that means is God cannot make us do anything. He can influence our choices but can't make us choose anything. We are responsible for every action, word, and choice we make. Nothing and no one can force us to do or say anything. We are influenced by everything around us. Every person around us, every single thing we see, hear, smell, taste, and touch, influences us in some way. The question is, do we want good or bad influences? That's a huge question. We all need good influences in our lives to help us make good choices. But usually, it's more fun to have bad influences. Or is it? When you have bad influences, you do bad things, and they have negative consequences. Those consequences could be physical, mental, emotional, financial, and many others. Then, usually, you do more bad things to cover up the feelings you got from doing the other bad things. And before you know it, that becomes life. You are constantly lying to yourself and those around you, hiding your real emotions, and pushing your inner wounds deep down inside yourself. Then you numb yourself so it doesn't hurt as much.

I'm going to explain the steps we go through when we are stuck in this pattern of life. See if they make sense to you. I know all about them. I was stuck in this rut for a long time. Understand that when I say *bad*, I mean "sin." To sin is to go against God's will for our lives. Because of free will, we can do whatever we want, but God has a plan for our lives, and when we go against that plan, we sin.

It says in Romans 3:23, "All of us have sinned and fall short of the glory of God." (Version NIV)

In other words, we all do bad things, and that makes each one of us equal. When you sin, or do something bad, there is a mental process and emotional response. Every action in life, good or bad, has a mental process and emotional response. With the act of sinning, the mental process is guilt. You thought about doing something and acted on that thought; now you know what you did was

CHOICES

wrong, and you know you are guilty. The emotional response to sin is shame. After you mentally process guilt, you feel ashamed for what you did or are doing. Whether you realize it or not, you always feel shame. We don't always allow the feeling of shame to present itself in us. We try to push it deep down inside, but it always affects us in some way. When you combine the mental process guilt with the emotional response shame, you end up with regret:

$$guilt + shame = regret$$

You know what you did was wrong, you feel bad about it, and now you wish you hadn't done it. You wish you could take it back, but you can't. So you start to blame others and make excuses. After that, you will receive some sort of punishment. Every choice we make has a consequence, good or bad. There are many kinds of punishment, but the most common is self-punishment. You beat yourself up for the horrible things you've done. You might feel worthless and depressed. Then you feel upset and empty, and there is a void that you need to fill. So to comfort yourself, to fill that void, you might get drunk, do some drugs, overeat, stay busy in the garden, watch TV, or whatever makes you happy for a moment or takes your mind off things. Instead of turning to God and asking for help, we turn to something else to give us relief for a moment.

I call this the spiral of fear. You do something you know you shouldn't have done, and that is knowing you are guilty. You feel bad for doing it; you are ashamed of yourself. Then you wish you hadn't done it; you feel regret. Then you start to make excuses for it and blame other people. Then you might go to jail or receive a simple slap on the wrist. But regardless, you will beat yourself up for what you've done; you will receive punishment. Then you will feel an emptiness, a void inside you, and you will sin again. You will get caught in the spiral of fear at some point in life. The longer you are in this spiral, the easier it becomes. After a while, you don't feel anything anymore, and you're barely alive.

Spiral of Fear

Evil is the only reason there are any bad influences in this world. The word *evil* is *live* backward. That is exactly what evil has done. It has taught us to live backward. Evil is what separates us from God. God is holy, he is perfect, and he is pure. God cannot have evil in his presence. We cannot be in his presence because we are evil. We would die if we were in God's presence.

In the beginning, after God created the universe, the earth, and everything on the earth, he created a man. God made the man in his own image and breathed the breath of life into his nostrils. God saw that the man needed a partner. He put the man into a deep sleep, removed one of his ribs, and created a woman. God created a garden for the man and woman to live in and take care of. God wasn't always in the garden with them, but he would walk and talk with them. Imagine learning how to live straight from the mouth of the one who created life. Life would be much easier if we had God by our side, teaching us what we need to do. And we would live in a perfect world and wouldn't have the knowledge of evil. We would only have the knowledge that God breathed into us when the man, Adam, was created.

Where did evil come from? In the garden that God created, the Garden of Eden, two trees were in the middle. God told Adam and Eve they could eat from any tree in the garden except from the Tree of the Knowledge of Good and Evil. If they ate from that tree, they would surely die. There was also the Tree of Life. They would have had eternal life if they had eaten from the Tree of Life. God gave Adam and Eve one commandment: "Do not eat from the Tree of the Knowledge of Good and Evil." (Gen 2:17a, NIV)

But the question is, why give them that choice? Why not just live with them in harmony and have no worries? Earlier in this chapter, I talked about free will. That is the ability to make our own choices. The real question is, why do we have free will? If we are going to give God a chance in our lives, we need to understand what free will is. God isn't forcing us to love him. He wants us to choose to love him. For us to be able to choose to love him, we have to be able to make our own choices, which means we have to have free will.

God had a plan for all of humanity, as well as each one of us, since before he created anything. God knows all, sees all, is everywhere, and he is in total control. We can only see through our life, which is for less than 120 years. We have no idea what is happening anywhere else in the world or what others are thinking. But we still question God and the way he does things. Obviously, we are more intelligent than God, so why should we listen to him? Humanity is God's teenager. We think we know it all and God is just some made-up myth that makes no sense. The Bible says that we are children of God, and we sure act like it.

In the Garden of Eden, many trees produced fruit. Adam and Eve took care of them and ate from them. God had given them everything they needed. They loved God and only wanted to do what he told them to. But then this guy named Satan slithered into the picture. The first thing Satan did is question God. Then he doubted God's truth and made his ways sound better.

Satan said, "Did God say that?" Then he said, "You won't die, and you will gain wisdom and be like God."

They listened to Satan, immediately becoming self-aware and realizing they were naked. Before that, they were innocent and blameless, just like a child. Then they sewed fig leaves together to cover themselves because of the feeling of shame. They were ashamed of their naked bodies. Then they heard God walking through the garden, and he called out to Adam. Adam hid from God because he was naked and knew his actions were wrong. He knew he was guilty.

God said to Adam, "Where are you?" (Gen 3:9-13, NIV)

Adam said, "I heard you in the garden, and I was afraid because I was naked."

God asked, "Who told you that you were naked? Did you eat from the tree I told you not to?"

Adam responded, "The woman, who you gave to me, she gave me the fruit, and I ate."

God said to Eve, "What is this that you have done?"

Eve said, "The serpent deceived me, and I ate."

God cursed the serpent, the man, and the woman.

Those curses are what we live with to this very day. And we still have Satan questioning God, which causes us to doubt God. Then Satan tempts us to do what he wants us to do.

Think about what happens when something comes up in your own life that you know is something you shouldn't do. Usually, you first agree that it's a bad idea and name the reasons why it's a bad idea. Then there are a few reasons why it might not be the best idea, but it would probably be okay. Right then, if you don't turn to God and ask for help, you will give in. That is what Satan does. He questions everything God does, everything that is good, and he makes everything that is bad sound like a good idea. If you look at what

Adam went through after he gave in to Satan, it's exactly what we still go through. Adam experienced the spiral of fear. Satan tempts us, and he doesn't give up easily. After we give in, he condemns us for sinning. We gain shame, guilt, and everything that comes with them from sin.

God does not condemn us for the things we do. He calls out our name, just like he did when Adam hid from him. The question is, do you continue to hide, or do you answer his call? Will you stop hiding your sins, confess what you've done, and ask for forgiveness? That is repenting. Repenting is feeling sincere regret or remorse about your wrongdoings or sins. It is a change of heart and mind that brings us closer to God. We are born onto a path where we are walking away from God. We have our backs turned toward him. If we repent, confess our sins, and ask for forgiveness, God will forgive us. When God forgives us, he erases every sin we ever committed. They are gone, trashed, vanished, kaput. (Source: Oxford languages)

I want us to understand the walk we are truly on. Reading the book of Exodus in the Bible is an excellent comparison of our lives. So in the next chapter, first, we will get a good understanding of what was going on during Exodus. Then we will see how that compares to the beginning of humanity's story, starting in the Garden of Eden. We will dive right in, and hopefully, this will give you a new perspective.

First, we need to understand that God's plan for humanity was taking place. God had a plan to reconnect himself to humanity, and

CHOICES

it started with a man named Abram. God called out to Abram, and Abram listened and followed everything God said. Then he praised God for all his blessings and believed every promise God made to him. The first thing God told him to do was to leave his homeland and travel to a land called Canaan. Abram was seventy-five years old at that time. He packed up all of his and his wife's belongings, and his nephew Lot came with them. They traveled to Canaan without knowing what would happen but fully trusting God. When they entered Canaan, God promised Abram that he would give this land to his descendants. Canaan would eventually become the city of Jerusalem, also known as the Promised Land.

Abram's wife, Sarai, was barren, and God promised Abram he would have descendants as numerous as the stars. When Abram was ninety-nine years old, Sarai gave birth to a son. She named him Isaac. *Isaac* means "one who laughs." They were so happy and thankful to be blessed with a son. God changed Sarai's name to Sara, and Abram, God named Abraham. *Sara* means "noble woman," and *Abraham* means "father of many." They listened to God and did what he told them to do, and because of that, God blessed them and forgave them for their mistakes. At this point in the history of humanity, God hadn't given the ten commandments, so people didn't know what was right or wrong. Abraham and Sara either listened to God or they didn't. They didn't have any rules.

Abraham's son, Isaac, had two sons, Esau and Jacob. Jacob did a lot of mean things to Esau while they grew up. When Jacob was one hundred years old, Esau was coming to meet him. Jacob was very scared of what Esau might do. During the night, Jacob sent his two wives, eleven sons, and all their possessions away. He was all alone. That night a man wrestled with Jacob until daybreak. The man saw he couldn't defeat Jacob, so he struck the socket of Jacob's hip, and it was dislocated.

The man said, "Let me go."

Jacob replied, "I will not let you go unless you bless me."

The man asked, "What is your name?"

He answered, "Jacob."

"No longer will your name be Jacob," the man told him, "but Israel, because you have fought with God and man and have prevailed."

Israel means "wrestles with God." Jacob, whose name became Israel, would become the father of the Israelite nation. The Israelite nation would receive all the blessings God promised to Abraham, Isaac, and Jacob.

While Jacob was still alive, all his descendants, seventy of them, moved into Egypt. The pharaoh, or ruler of Egypt, gave Jacob and his descendants the best region of land in Egypt. The pharaoh's name was Ramesses II. Ramesses II and the Israelites had a great relationship with each other. When Ramesses II died and a new pharaoh took his place, everything changed. The new pharaoh didn't know anything about the Israelites. He saw them as foreign people taking over his land. He was going to make life as hard on them as possible.

Satan makes our lives as hard as possible because he wants our attention to be on anything other than God. We will understand this better in the next chapter. Every single one of us needs to understand where we are in this life and where we are going to end up in the afterlife.

Plagues

The first book in the Bible is Genesis. *Genesis* means "the origin or mode of formation of something." The first words in Genesis are "In the beginning . . ." The second book in the Bible is Exodus. *Exodus* means "a mass departure of people." (Source: Oxford languages)

In the book of Exodus, God's people—they are the Israelites—became slaves to the Egyptians. The pharaoh that took the place of Ramesses II oppressed the Israelites. He put foremen over them and forced them to do hard labor. But the more he oppressed them, the more they multiplied. The Egyptians thought the Israelites were taking over the land and began to hate them. The pharaoh ordered the Egyptians to throw every son born to the Israelites into the Nile River. The daughters could live, but the sons had to die.

While all this was happening, one of the Israelite women gave birth to a son. She put him in a basket and hid him behind reeds in the Nile River. The daughter of the pharaoh found the child. She wanted to keep him and raise him. She named the child *Moses*, which means "to pull or draw out." (Source: Wikipedia)

CHOICES

The pharaoh's daughter needed someone to nurse the child. Moses's sister asked the pharaoh's daughter if she should get an Israelite woman to nurse the child.

The pharaoh's daughter said, "Go."

She called Moses's mom, and Moses's real mom nursed him. The pharaoh's daughter raised Moses in the pharaoh's palace, but he knew he belonged to the Israelites. One day being a grown-up, Moses saw an Egyptian beating one of his people. Moses killed the Egyptian. Moses had to leave Egypt so that they wouldn't kill him. For forty years, he lived in the land of Midian. While he was gone, the pharaoh died, and another pharaoh, who didn't know Moses, took his place.

The Israelites groaned and cried out to God because of the slave labor. God heard them and called Moses to go back to Egypt and set his people free. Moses was scared to go back to Egypt. God showed his power and strength to Moses. God would do the work; Moses just had to follow God's call. Moses thought he wasn't good at talking. God called Moses's brother Aaron to go along and do the talking. Moses would lead them into battle, Aaron would do the talking, and God would do the fighting. God gave Moses and Aaron all the abilities and words they needed to do what God asked them to do. The only thing they had to do was listen to God and do what he told them. He gave both of them meaning and purpose, and God showed his love for them and all his people through his actions. Ten plagues happened against Egypt in the book of Exodus. Plagues cause continual trouble or disease. God told Moses and Aaron to go to the pharaoh and tell him to release his people.

PLAGUES

Think about that. God was telling them to go straight into the enemy's land and tell him to release the people he made into slaves. What would it take for you to go directly to a very powerful leader and tell him to release these prisoners? It takes a lot more than just courage. That is called faith. Faith is complete trust or confidence in God. (Source: Oxford languages)

You genuinely believe God is with you, and he will do whatever is necessary to help you get through life and all the troubles that come with it. The pharaoh didn't know God and had no reason to listen to him or anyone talking about him. That's exactly how it is for anyone who doesn't know God. We don't know God and have no reason to listen to him. That means God has to do some drastic things to get our attention. But regardless of what happens, we have to choose to either accept Christ, who is our connection to God, or not. That is the most important choice we will ever make.

Moses and Aaron went to the pharaoh and told him that the Lord God said, "Release my people into the wilderness so they can hold a feast to me." (Exo 5:1-2, NIV)

The pharaoh asked them, "Who is the Lord, and why should I obey him? I do not know the Lord and will not release the Israelites."

Then the pharaoh made life harder for the Israelites. He took away the straw they used to build bricks. They were using bricks to build buildings, and now they had to find straw to make the bricks. But the pharaoh told them they still had to make the same number of bricks daily. They had to do the same amount of work but with much less resources.

CHOICES

If you take one tiny step toward God, you can expect the same thing to happen. Satan will make your life harder. He does whatever he can to turn your attention away from God. His favorite thing to do is make you feel like you're not good enough. Satan makes you feel like you're worse than most people and shouldn't bother God. Satan wants you to think that God's too busy and you don't deserve his love because you're not good enough. Understand that God loves you with unconditional love. No matter what you have done, God will forgive you if you put your faith in Jesus Christ. Jesus Christ has taken your place. He took the punishment each one of us deserves. When Satan makes your life hard, ask God for help, and remember that God loves you, not because of what you have done, but because you are his child.

God told Moses and Aaron that the pharaoh would ask for a sign when they talked to him again. God told Aaron to throw his staff on the ground and it would turn into a snake. Aaron threw his staff down on the ground in front of the pharaoh, and it turned into a snake. When the pharaoh saw this, he summoned the wise men, sorcerers, and magicians of Egypt, and they turned their staffs into snakes through their secret arts. But Aaron's snake ate their snakes. The pharaoh didn't listen to Moses and Aaron when they told him to let the Israelites go. Now it was time for God to start getting serious.

God told Moses and Aaron to meet the pharaoh in the morning when he went to the Nile River. God told them to say to the pharaoh, "'I have said release my people so they may serve me in the wil-

PLAGUES

derness, but you have not done this. By this, you will know that I am the Lord. I will strike the water of the Nile with the staff in my hand, and it will turn into blood. Fish in the Nile will die, the Nile will stink, and the Egyptians will be unable to drink water from the Nile.' Take your staff and stretch it over Egypt's water—over their rivers, canals, ponds, and reservoirs—so it becomes blood. There will be blood everywhere in Egypt, even in the wooden and stone vessels." (Exo 7:16b-19, NIV)

In front of the pharaoh, Aaron lifted the same staff that turned into a snake and struck the water in the Nile. There was blood everywhere in Egypt. The fish in the Nile died, the Nile began to stink, and the Egyptians couldn't drink water from the Nile. The pharaoh summoned the magicians, and they turned the Nile into blood. The pharaoh ignored God and all that he had said. The Egyptians had to dig next to the Nile for water to drink. The magicians only turned the Nile to blood, nothing else, no other waters. Why wouldn't they make the water fresh and clean? Why wouldn't they reverse what God did? Most likely, they were doing some trick. The magicians, sorcerers, and wise men were probably putting dye in the Nile. Turning the water to blood was the first plague of ten.

One week passed since the Lord struck the Nile. God told Moses to go to the pharaoh and tell him, "This is what the Lord says 'Release my people so they may serve me. But if you refuse to release them, I will plague your territory with frogs. They will come up into your house, into your bedroom, onto your bed, into the houses of your servants and your people, and into your ovens and kneading troughs. Frogs will come up against you, your people, and all your servants.'" (Exo 8:1-4, 8:6-8, NIV)

Moses and Aaron went to the pharaoh, and Aaron extended his staff over the waters of Egypt. Frogs came out and covered the land. Again, the magicians did the same thing with their secret arts.

But this time, the pharaoh summoned Moses and Aaron and said, "Pray to the Lord that he will take the frogs away, and I will release the people that they may sacrifice to the Lord."

Moses told the pharaoh that the only place that frogs would remain would be in the Nile. Moses and Aaron left the pharaoh, prayed to God, and all the frogs in the land died. The Egyptians had to pile them in countless heaps, and the whole land stank. But when the pharaoh saw relief, he didn't let the people go, which the Lord said would happen.

God said to Moses, "Say to Aaron, 'Stretch out your staff and strike the dust of the land, and it will become gnats in all the land of Egypt.'" (Exo 8:16-19, NIV)

Aaron stretched out his hand with his staff, and the dust became gnats and covered the humans and the animals in all the land of Egypt. The magicians tried to bring gnats out of the dust with their secret ways, but they couldn't do it.

They said to the pharaoh, "This is the finger of God."

But the pharaoh didn't listen to them. The magicians had illusions and tricks to perform their version of the other plagues, but they could not do this. But still, the pharaoh wouldn't listen to God. That was the third plague, and it was the last plague that would affect the Israelites. The first three plagues affected the entire land, both the Egyptians and the Israelites. But now God separated his people, the Israelites, from those opposed to him, the Egyptians.

I'm going to stop here and take a closer look at these first three plagues. I want to compare the fall of man, Genesis chapter 3, and the first three plagues, Exodus chapters 7–8. Genesis 3:1–6 tells us that a serpent came into the garden, questioned God's authority, gave doubt to the man and woman, and then they didn't listen to what God had commanded them. Exodus 7:8–13 tells us that God turned Aaron's staff into a snake. The magicians questioned God's authority, and the pharaoh didn't listen to what God had commanded him to do. By the way, you can read these verses in any Bible and see how similar they are and that both stories are five verses long.

In Genesis 3:1–6, Adam and Eve were tricked by Satan and didn't listen to God. They lost their source of strength and power, God. They still had blood in their veins but lost everything else. God gave them a perfect life, and they chose to lose it. Now they would have to learn how to live without their source of life, which is God. Adam and Eve would have to dig in the ground to grow their food because God would no longer give them food. They had to work for it.

In Exodus 7:14–24, the pharaoh was tricked by the magicians, sorcerers, and wise men and didn't listen to God. The Egyptians lost their source of strength and power, the Nile River. They had blood everywhere but no water to drink. The pharaoh was a powerful man and lived a luxurious life. But things were about to get very hard. The Egyptians had to dig in the ground next to the Nile to get water to drink. The only thing the Egyptians, Adam, Eve, or any of us would need to do to have a better life is listen to God. God was judging the power the pharaoh had. God showed him how easily he could take his power away. God judged Adam, Eve, and the serpent by cursing them.

God also proved that the gods of Egypt were nonsense. The god of the Nile was Hapi. The Egyptians believed Hapi caused the Nile to flood annually. The flood made the soil fertile, and the Egyptians could plant and grow crops. The image of Hapi had a fat belly, drooping breasts, a loincloth, and a ceremonial beard. This image represents the fertility of the river and its richness. The god Khnum was the source and guardian of the Nile. He also created children at a potter's wheel and put them in a mother's womb. Khnum created gods as well. The Egyptians believed that the Nile River was the bloodstream of Osiris, god of the underworld, and he was reborn each year when the river flooded. So God made the Nile into an actual bloodstream and showed the Egyptians how weak their man-made gods were.

In Genesis 3:7–8, Adam and Eve gained two new gods, and they had to please them. Those gods were guilt and shame. Anything that becomes more important than the Lord God or gains your full attention becomes a god. They sewed fig leaves together to try to please shame and hid from God to try to please guilt. The knowledge of good and evil they had gained was taking over their world and ruining everything.

PLAGUES

In Exodus 8:1–15, frogs were taking over the land and ruining everything. The pharaoh couldn't get the frogs to leave, so he decided to try to please God and make a deal with him. The pharaoh would allow the Israelites to offer sacrifices to the Lord if the Lord removed the frogs. Every god the pharaoh knew, he had to try to please. The Lord God doesn't need to be pleased. The Israelites made sacrifices to God to cover their sins, and they gave offerings to God to show gratitude for everything he did for them.

Satan doesn't have any power. Neither did the wise men, sorcerers, and magicians. They all have tricks, lies, and manipulation. God has the power. We have choices to make, and Satan deceives us. Also, the gods of Egypt didn't have any power. Frogs represented fertility, and so did Heket (Heqet), the goddess of frogs. She personified birth, generations, and fertility. She was married to Khnum, who made children and gods. But where was the goddess of the frogs when they were running totally out of control and everywhere? And Sobek was the god of crocodiles or reptiles. He was the god of wetlands, marshes, and other wet areas. Sobek was a protective deity. He protected against the dangers presented by the Nile River. He was also associated with power, fertility, and military prowess. Sobek is said to have created the Nile with his sweat. Where was he to fight against God and protect the Egyptians? The Egyptians had to kill the reptiles they praised. Neither their gods nor their magicians could do anything to stop God from ruining their land. The only thing they needed to do was listen to God and release his people.

CHOICES

In Genesis 3:9-24, evil spread to every living creature that God created from dust. That would have been Adam, Eve, and every animal. God kicked Adam and Eve out of the garden and allowed evil to spread everywhere. Satan doesn't have the power to spread evil; he can only do evil. Now everything in the world would be completely different.

In Exodus 8:16-19, the dust turned into a small insect and covered every human and animal. The magicians admitted this was the finger of God. They didn't have the power to do that. They didn't have the power to do anything close to that. God showed the Egyptians he was more powerful than their sorcerers, wise men, and magicians. God judged the power of every possible strength the Egyptians had. But the pharaoh still felt like he was more powerful than God. Geb was the god of the earth. He had power over earthquakes, farming, fertility, and healing. Again, God showed Egypt that their gods had no power.

I'm going to go back to the plagues and continue from the fourth plague. God said to Moses, "Confront the pharaoh in the morning as he goes to the water and say to him, 'The Lord says, Let my people go so they can worship me. If you don't, I will send swarms of flies on you and your officials, on your people, and into your houses. The houses of the Egyptians will be full. Even the ground will be covered with flies. But I will deal differently with the land of Goshen, where my people live; no swarms of flies will be there so that you know I am in this land. I will make a distinction between my people and your people. This will be my sign tomorrow.'" (Exo 8:20-32, NIV)

PLAGUES

Dense swarms of flies poured into the pharaoh's palace, the houses of his officials, and throughout Egypt. Flies ruined the land.

The pharaoh summoned Moses and said, "Sacrifice to your God here in the land."

Moses said, "The sacrifices we offer God would be detestable to the Egyptians, and they would stone us to death. We must take a three-day journey."

The pharaoh said, "I will let you go to offer sacrifices to your God, but you must not go far."

Moses agreed to this and said, "As soon as I leave, I will pray to the Lord, and the flies will leave tomorrow. But do not act deceitfully again."

Moses prayed, and the flies were gone. Not a single fly remained. But again, the pharaoh wouldn't let God's people go.

After that, the Lord said to Moses, "Go to the pharaoh and say to him, 'This is what the Lord says; "Let my people go worship me. If you don't, God will bring a terrible plague on your livestock in the field—on your horses, donkeys, sheep, and goats." But God will make a distinction between the livestock of Israel and Egypt so that not a single animal of the Israelites will die.'" (Exo 9:1-4,9:6-7, NIV)

The next day the Lord did this. All the livestock of the Egyptians died. For the fifth plague, God killed every animal the Egyptians owned. The pharaoh investigated and found that not even one animal of the Israelites died. But he still wouldn't let the people go.

God said to Moses and Aaron, "Take handfuls of soot from a furnace, and toss it in the air in the presence of the pharaoh. It will become fine dust over the whole land of Egypt, and festering boils will break out on people and animals throughout the land." (Exo 9:8-12, NIV)

Moses did this in front of the pharaoh, and festering boils broke out on people and animals. The magicians couldn't stand in front of Moses because of the boils on them. That was the sixth plague. But the pharaoh wouldn't listen to Moses and Aaron.

For the seventh plague, God said to Moses, "Get up early, confront the pharaoh and say, 'This is what the Lord says, "Let my people go, or this time I will send the full force of my plagues against you and your officials and your people, so you may know there is no one like me in all the earth. You still set yourself against my people and will not let them go. Therefore, I will send the worst hailstorm that has ever fallen on Egypt tomorrow. Give an order to bring your livestock and everything you have in the field to a place of shelter because the hail will fall on every person and animal that has not been brought in, and they will die."'" (Exo 9:13-14,9:17-35, NIV)

The officials who feared the word of the Lord brought their slaves and livestock inside, but the others didn't and left them in the field. God told Moses to stretch out his hand toward the sky so that hail would fall on people, animals, and everything growing in the fields of Egypt. Moses did this, and God sent thunder and hail, and lightning flashed down to the ground. It was the worst storm in Egypt since it had become a nation. Throughout Egypt, the hail struck everything in the fields, both people and animals. It beat down everything growing in the fields and stripped every tree. Goshen, where the Israelites lived, was the only place it didn't hail.

PLAGUES

The pharaoh summoned Moses and Aaron, saying, "This time I have sinned. The Lord is in the right, and my people and I are in the wrong. Pray to the Lord. We have had enough thunder and hail. I will let you go. You don't have to stay any longer."

Moses said, "I will pray when I leave the city, and the thunder and hail will stop. But I know you and your officials still do not fear the Lord God."

When the pharaoh saw the rain, hail, and thunder stopped, he sinned again. He would not let the Israelites go. God had said that would happen.

Moses and Aaron went to the pharaoh and said, "This is what the Lord, God of the Hebrews, says, 'How long will you refuse to humble yourself before me? Let my people go so that they may worship me. If you refuse to let them go, I will bring locusts into your country tomorrow. They will cover the face of the ground so that it cannot be seen. They will devour the little you have left after the hail, including every tree growing in your fields. They will fill all of your houses, something neither your parents nor ancestors have seen from the day they settled this land until now.'" (Exo 10:3-9, 10:11, 10:13-20, NIV)

Then Moses left the pharaoh.

The pharaoh's officials said to him, "How long will this man be a snare to us? Let the people go. Don't you see that Egypt is ruined?"

The pharaoh brought Moses and Aaron back and said, "Go, worship your God, but tell me who will be going."

Moses answered, "We will be going with our young and old, our sons and daughters, and with our flocks and herds because we are to celebrate a festival to the Lord."

CHOICES

The pharaoh said, "No! Have only the men go since that's what you've been asking for." Then Moses and Aaron were driven from the pharaoh's presence.

Moses stretched out his staff, and the Lord made an east wind blow across the land all that day and night. By morning, the wind had brought locusts. Never before had there been such a plague of locusts, nor will there ever be again. They covered all the ground until it was black. They devoured everything left after the hail—everything growing in the fields and the fruit on the trees. Nothing green remained on trees or plants in all the land of Egypt.

The pharaoh summoned Moses and Aaron and said, "I have sinned, now forgive my sin once more, and pray to the Lord your God to take this deadly plague away."

Moses left the pharaoh and prayed to the Lord. And the Lord changed the wind to a strong west wind, which caught the locusts and carried them into the Red Sea. Not a locust was left anywhere in Egypt. Again, the pharaoh would not let the people go, just as the Lord had said. That was the eighth plague.

For the ninth plague, the Lord told Moses, "Stretch out your hand toward the sky so that darkness spreads over Egypt, a darkness that can be felt." (Exo 10:21-26, 10:28-29, NIV)

So Moses stretched his hand toward the sky, and total darkness covered Egypt for three days. No one could see anyone else or move about for three days. But all the Israelites had light where they lived.

The pharaoh summoned Moses and said, "Go, worship the Lord. Even your women and children may go, only leave your flocks and herds behind."

Moses said, "You must allow us to have sacrifices and offerings to present to the Lord our God. All of our livestock must go. Until we get there, we will not know what we are to use to worship the Lord."

The pharaoh said, "Get out of my sight! Do not appear before me again! The day you see my face, you will die."

Moses replied, "Just as you say, I will never appear before you again."

God told Moses, "I will bring one more plague on the pharaoh and Egypt. After that, he will let you go, and when he does, he will drive you out completely." (Exo 11:1, 11:4-9, 12:3, 12:6-7, 12:12-13, 12:21-24, 12:29, 12:31-33, NIV)

Moses went to the pharaoh and said, "This is what the Lord says: 'About midnight I will go throughout Egypt. Every firstborn son in Egypt will die, from the firstborn son of the pharaoh to the firstborn son of the female slave and all the firstborns of the cattle. There will be loud wailing throughout Egypt, worse than it has ever been or ever will be again. But among the Israelites, not a dog will bark. Then you will know that the Lord distinguishes between Egypt and Israel.'"

Then Moses, hot with anger, left the pharaoh. The pharaoh would not let the Israelites leave his country.

God told Moses, "Tell the Israelites that each man is to take a lamb for his household. All the members of the community must slaughter them. Then they are to take some of the blood and put it on the tops and sides of the doorframes of their houses. I will

CHOICES

pass through Egypt and strike down every firstborn of both people and animals, and I will bring judgment on all the gods of Egypt. The blood will be a sign for you on the houses where you are, and when I see the blood, I will pass over you. No destructive plague will touch you when I strike Egypt."

Moses told the Israelites, "Go at once and select a lamb and slaughter the Passover lamb. Take a bunch of hyssop [which is a plant], dip it into the blood in the basin, and put some blood on the top and both sides of the doorframe. Not one of you shall go out of the door of your house until morning. When the Lord goes through to strike down Egyptians, he will see the blood and pass over that doorway, and he will not allow the destroyer to enter your houses and strike you down."

At midnight the Lord struck down all the firstborn sons in Egypt, from the pharaoh who sat on the throne to the prisoner who sat in the dungeon and all the livestock.

During the night, the pharaoh summoned Moses and Aaron and said, "Up! Leave my people, you and all the Israelites! Go, worship the Lord as you have requested, take your flocks and herds, as you have said, and go. And also bless me."

The Egyptians urged the Israelites to leave their country. "For otherwise," they said, "we will all die."

Now the Israelites were free, not because of what they had done but because of what God had done for them.

To read these stories in full, go to Exodus chapters 7 through 12. Every time the Bible says, "The Lord hardened the pharaoh's heart," it's saying that God gave him a choice. If the pharaoh had chosen to let the Israelites leave, he would have been listening to God. When we listen to God, our hearts soften. When we choose to do what is best for ourselves and hurt others, we are not listening to God, which is having a hardened heart. Because we have free will, God cannot make any choices for us. It is saying that God gave the pharaoh a choice, and the pharaoh chose to harden his own heart.

During the fall of humanity and the first plague, Adam, Eve, and the Egyptians lost their source of power and strength. They were still alive and had blood in their veins, but life would be much more complicated. When Adam and Eve turned away from the one true God, they immediately had other gods to try to please. They were the only kind of gods the pharaoh knew, ones you had to please. The pharaoh tried to do the same thing with the one true God. He tried to please him then he wouldn't have to listen to him. Because Adam and Eve chose to sin, God allowed evil to spread throughout the earth and cover every living thing. Because the pharaoh wouldn't listen to God, small insects spread throughout the entire land and covered every living thing.

In Genesis 4:1–16, Adam and Eve had two sons, Cain and Abel. Abel kept flocks, and Cain worked the soil. Cain offered some of the fruits of the soil to the Lord. Abel also offered some fat portions from his flocks. God accepted Abel's offering but not Cain's. Understand that God covered Adam and Eve with the skin of an animal in the garden. God covered their shame with an animal, and Abel understood that. God had also cursed the ground because Adam had eaten from the tree.

CHOICES

God said, "Now, through painful toil, you will eat from the soil. It will produce thorns and thistles." (Gen 3:17b-18a, NIV)

Abel offered something back to God that God gave as a gift. Cain offered something to God that God had cursed.

God told Cain, "If you do what is right, will it not be accepted?" (Gen 4:7a, NIV)

If Cain would've offered fat portions like his brother, everything would've been fine. Instead, Cain killed his brother, Abel. Cain wanted to do things his own way, not God's way.

God told Cain, "Your brother's blood cries to me from the ground. Now you are under a curse, no longer will the ground produce crops for you. You will be a restless wanderer." (Gen 4:10-12, NIV)

God drove Cain out of his presence, from the land of Eden to the land of Nod. God made a distinction between those who listened to him and those who chose to do things their own way.

In the fourth plague, God sent swarms of flies into Egypt, into all their houses and all over the ground. The flies ruined the land. But not a single fly was in Goshen, the land the Israelites lived in. God distinguished between his people and the Egyptians. The pharaoh told Moses he would let them go to offer sacrifices to God, but they couldn't go far. The pharaoh still wanted to do things his way. Even though God knew the pharaoh was lying, God still removed the flies. God could have left each plague like it was and kept adding plagues. But that would have been too much for the Egyptians. When God cursed Cain to be a wanderer, he put a mark on him so that no one who found him would kill him. That is called grace.

PLAGUES

Grace is undeserved favor. God still helps people even when they've sinned. You sin, God judges you, you listen to him and receive his judgment, and then he helps you even though it was your choice to sin. During this plague, God showed that he was judging the Egyptians, who did things their own way. But he showed grace to his people, who listened to him. Even when we sin God loves us and helps us. (Source: Compassion.com)

That plague also showed the Egyptians that God was in total control of everything in nature. Khepri was the Egyptian god of the sunrise and also represented the creation and renewal of life. Egyptians pictured Khepri with a human body and the head of a scarab beetle. A scarab beetle is a dung beetle that lays eggs in a pile of dung. They roll dung into balls that look like the sun rising. Young beetles come out of dung piles, and dung piles are nothingness. The Egyptians believed that each day, Khepri made the sun from nothing. That's why they connected him to the creation and renewal of life. He had the head of an insect, and the Egyptians connected him to the creation of the world. But how could he create anything if he didn't have control of nature?

In Genesis 4:25, Eve gave birth to another son and said, "God has granted me another son in place of Abel." (Version NIV)

God sent Adam and Eve another son shortly after Abel's death to heal the heartache. God blessed them because they were now staying focused on him. Their son, whose name was Seth, also had a son. At that time, people began to call on the Lord. God blesses those who follow him, and others notice that. Those who don't follow him will lose what they already have. All they have to do is call on him, and he will bless them. For the fifth plague, all the livestock of the Egyptians died. The pharaoh sent men to investigate and found that not even one of the Israelite's livestock had died. Now they could see that God was blessing his people and judging Egypt. God was blessing the Israelites, and the Egyptians were losing what they already had.

God judged the Egyptian's possessions and their way of gaining possessions. The livestock would have been their primary possessions and way to gain other possessions. They would have helped them farm. God also judged the Egyptian god Hathor. Hathor is represented as a cow because she is pictured as giving sustenance to her people. She is also displayed as a beautiful woman with cow horns on her head. Ptah was said to be the god that created the universe, and his symbol was a bull. And cows and bulls were the holiest of animals in Egypt. During this plague, they lost all their horses, donkeys, camels, cattle, sheep, and goats. They had nothing to sustain them or get back what they lost.

Genesis 6:1 says that humans began to increase in number on the earth, and in verse 3, God says, "My spirit will not contend with humans forever; they are flesh. Their years shall be one hundred and twenty." (Version NIV)

Before that time, people were living longer lives. Adam lived to be 930 years old. But because evil was in humans, they had to have an earlier end. God decided 120 years was long enough for humans to be on this earth. Humans increased physically, and God made a righteous judgment on the number of physical years they would have.

The sixth plague was the plague of boils. Because the pharaoh wouldn't listen to God, boils broke out on the skin of every Egyptian in the land. Now God judged them physically. He judged their way of life with flies swarming through all their buildings and land and taking away their possessions and ability to gain possessions. Flies are annoying, losing your livestock is devastating, and having boils all over your body hurts and feels horrible. God judged them physically, emotionally, and spiritually. Sekhmet is a warrior goddess as well as the goddess of healing. Egyptians often depicted her as a lion. Again, the Egyptians had no help, and the only thing that needed to happen was that the pharaoh set the Israelites free. Then all that would end, and everything would eventually be okay.

Also, in Genesis chapter 6, the sons of God had children with the daughters of men. Sons of God could be angels or devoutly religious men. Devoutly religious men would be entirely focused on God. At that time there were no rules or laws to live by. You either knew who God was or you didn't. But whoever they were, they shouldn't have been having relations with these women. Angels obviously shouldn't be having children with humans, and men focused on God should be very careful about whom they marry and have children with. When God leads you, you can admit you're wrong and then listen to God, and he will cover you; he will protect you. But that wasn't happening then, and people were getting farther away from God.

CHOICES

The seventh plague was hail. At this point, God told the pharaoh that he could have sent a plague and wiped them off the earth, but he didn't because the purpose of the Egyptians was so God could show his power and have his name proclaimed throughout the whole world. You can read that and think it sounds crazy, but if people experience God's power and see his love, they turn toward him. When they turn toward him, they turn away from Satan. Then God can do all the things for them he has been doing for the Israelites. That happened in Egypt when he warned them of a hailstorm worse than had ever been seen before. The officials who believed him brought their slaves and livestock inside. But those who didn't believe him left them outside. God covered and protected those who obeyed him. During the hailstorm, the pharaoh admitted he was wrong, God was right, and the Egyptians were in the wrong. The pharaoh asked Moses to pray for him. Moses agreed to pray for him, but Moses said, "I know you and your officials still don't fear the Lord." But he prayed, God stopped the hailstorm, and the pharaoh wouldn't let the Israelites go. (Exo 9:30, NIV)

God judged Egypt because they weren't listening to him. They weren't doing what he told them to do. The hailstorm destroyed the flax and barley because the barley was headed and the flax was in bloom or budded. The wheat and spelt were still good because they ripened later. But the Egyptians had lost a lot of animals, slaves, produce, and time. The only thing they had to do was turn to God and obey him. That was beginning to make sense to some of the Egyptians. God also showed that the gods Nut, Seth, and Shu were

PLAGUES

meaningless and fake. Nut is the goddess of the sky and all heavenly bodies. Nut is the daughter of Shu, the god of the atmosphere and the air and supporter of the sky. Seth was the god of storms and lands. The big question is, which god is more powerful, and whom do you listen to—the God destroying everything or these gods allowing you to be destroyed?

In Genesis 6:5-7, God sees how wicked the human race has become. Every thought of the human heart is only to do evil all the time. God regrets creating humans and plans to eliminate every human being and every animal that breathes air. He plans to destroy everything except for the earth itself. During the seventh plague, God sent locusts into Egypt, and the locusts ate anything growing in the fields or on the trees that survived the hailstorm. The land was still there, but it was no longer producing life. The pharaoh asked Moses who would be going along to praise and worship the Lord. Moses said everyone, but he used a few more words than that. The pharaoh denied him and told him only the men could go. The pharaoh still wanted to have control and power. That is called pride. The pharaoh was satisfied with his accomplishments and wouldn't allow anyone to tell him what to do. He was trying to make a deal with God instead of obeying him. God judged the pride of the pharaoh and his people. Though they didn't have much left, they still wouldn't give up what they considered their control and power. The pharaoh's officials asked him, "How long will this man be a snare to us? Let the people go. Don't you realize Egypt is ruined?" (Exo 10:7, NIV)

CHOICES

The officials looked at Moses and Aaron as the reason for their problems. Though Moses and Aaron always said, "This is what the Lord says...," the Egyptians wanted to get rid of Moses and Aaron. They weren't concerned about the Lord. The god Osiris was the god of the underworld, and he was the ruler of the dead. He also had the power to grant life from the underworld, from vegetation to the annual flood of the Nile River. And he was the protector of crops.

In Genesis 6:8–22, God calls out to Noah and tells him to build an ark. God tells Noah he is going to destroy all of life with flood waters. God tells Noah exactly how to build the ark, whom to put in the ark, and what animals to take along. God doesn't leave out any details. But everyone else on earth has become entirely corrupt and couldn't understand why Noah would do something like this. They are blinded by the evil inside them, all around them, and their own evil actions, which are their choices.

The ninth plague was darkness, a darkness that could be felt. The Egyptians were literally blind for three days. They couldn't go anywhere, do anything, or see anyone. But in the land of the Israelites, there was light. The pharaoh told Moses to go worship the Lord and that even the women and children could go but leave the flocks and herds behind. Moses told the pharaoh they must take the flocks and herds to have sacrifices and offerings to give to the Lord.

The pharaoh ordered Moses, "Leave and never come back, or you will die." (Exo 10:28, NIV)

The pharaoh allowed the people to go but didn't allow them to praise and worship their God. He still wanted control. Now God was

PLAGUES

judging their spiritual blindness. He made them physically blind to show them they couldn't see the truth. The pharaoh fought against men, but his actual battle was against God. The pharaoh was blind to that, and God was trying to show it to him. The god of the sun was Ra, and he was the most-worshipped god in Egypt. Ra was the father of all creation.

Genesis 7:6-24 explains that flood waters came upon the earth, and every living thing was wiped out. Noah, his wife, his sons, and their families were the only people to survive. They survive because God calls out to Noah and tells him what to do, and Noah obeys God. Noah listens to what God says.

Everyone who ignores God dies, just like in the tenth plague. The firstborn or oldest son of every Egyptian died. God gave instructions to the Israelites, and they obeyed him. They listened to him. Not even a dog barked in the land of the Israelites, but there was loud wailing in Egypt. Finally, the pharaoh called Moses and said, "Go, get out of my land." Then the Israelites left Egypt and were no longer slaves.

In Exodus 1:22, at the beginning of Exodus, the pharaoh ordered his people to throw the male babies of the Israelites into the Nile. Now God judged them for doing that. God did not just kill a bunch of people for no reason. The Egyptians killed and mistreated the Israelites for 430 years. God is just, and he judged the Egyptians for all that they had done. Their god Min was the god of reproduction, and Heket, the goddess with a frog's head, was the goddess of fertility and birth.

CHOICES

Through the ten plagues, God set his people free from enslavement, gave Moses and all the Israelites a new life, and showed the Egyptians his power and the weakness of their gods. God showed how he protects, blesses, separates, and guides his people. Now the big question is, where are you in this life? Who do you follow? How do you get a better life, and what will that cost you?

Commandments

Why do the plagues or anything from the book of Exodus matter to us today? Because we are slaves in this life. We have many different gods all around us that we listen to, and they control us. We have many different excuses we give to ourselves and those around us as to why we do things that we know are killing us. We have a choice to listen to and obey God, but why would we bother doing that? We have our lives under control and going exactly how we want them to, so we don't need anyone to tell us what to do. We have all the power, control, and authority we need, so we don't need to listen to or obey anyone or anything. That's exactly why nothing is going how we want it to and we can't find happiness.

Believe it or not, our lives are the ten plagues. The first three plagues happen to everyone who has ever lived. The next three, plagues 4–6, happen to those who don't know God, the unrighteous. The next three, plagues 7–9, are personal, and the last plague is death. I want to take a deep look at these. I want you to understand this because it is real. I know it is because I experienced every one of these plagues except the last one. Thankfully, God got my attention before I died.

I want you to have the same opportunity. I am not a salesman trying to sell some crazy product or get rich and famous from my ideas. I'm a guy who was given a brand-new life because he listened to God. God called my name, and I said, "Here I am," and he did the rest. Life is a challenge, but if you can feel content, life looks and feels completely different. Give God a chance. He is calling your name. Say yes to him, and begin a new journey.

Earlier I explained that we gain a conscious mind around the age of six, but it doesn't fully develop until we are between eleven and thirteen. As soon as we can make our own choices, we choose to stop listening to any authoritative figure in our life. We listen to our friends. They are the same age as us and are experiencing the same kinds of things we are. Whether you believe in God or not, you stop listening to him as soon as you sin. That is the first thing we all do. As soon as we develop a conscious mind, we choose to do things our way, not God's, and start sinning. It's the same thing Adam and Eve did and also what the pharaoh did. We ignore God. Throughout our entire life, God calls out our names and tries to get our attention. I mean that for every single one of us. So the actual first step we take is ignoring God.

We are born separated from God because we have evil inside of us and all around us. We are living in two worlds at the same time. All around us, angels and demons are fighting and speaking to us. Some people can see into the spiritual world, but most of us only see this world in front of us. We are just like a frog. We can live on land and in the water. The land is this world, and the water is the spiritual world. Our choice is, do we focus on this world or the spiritual things? We have the knowledge of good and evil but have lost the wisdom of love. We can choose to do either good or evil, but our best option is to do things out of love. In the Garden of Eden, the only knowledge or wisdom Adam and Eve had was love. They knew the love God had for them, and they had that same love for him and each other.

Our version of love today is highly distorted. When someone gives us what we want them to give us, then we love them. We stop loving them as soon as they stop giving us what we want. Truly loving someone is giving up the things you want to help someone get what they need. Like a mother who gives up the life they wanted to help their baby have the life they need. We have a choice to either focus on the things of this world or turn to God and focus on him. Step 1 is ignoring God. We live between two worlds because we ignore him. Step 2 is living in and focusing on this world and the things of this world instead of God and the spiritual things.

Instead of kicking Adam and Eve out of the Garden of Eden and allowing sin to spread, God could have destroyed everything. Why has he allowed us to live like this for over six thousand years? One reason is that he had a plan for everything before time began. Another reason is that he loves each and every single one of us and wants as many of us as possible with him in heaven. God has

CHOICES

allowed the world and everything in it to stay in this bad condition. He wants us, every one of us, to choose to be with him. Instead of living life on our own, our own way, doing what we want, and having significant consequences, we can turn to God and follow him. But instead we turn to our urges and desires and follow them. We follow evil instead of God. Just like the dust turned into small insects and landed on every human and animal in the third plague, we have evil in us and all around us, so we follow it.

First we ignore God, then we turn away from him, and then we follow evil. That is the beginning of life for every human being ever born. We all follow different roads and paths; do different things; and have different goals and dreams, wants and desires; but all of us are disconnected from God and follow evil ways. When we are old enough to understand right and wrong, good and bad, and punishment and reward, we are old enough to choose to follow God. That happens between the ages of eleven and thirteen, when our conscious mind is fully developed. Some of us have a family that believes in God, and by eleven or twelve, we have faith in Jesus Christ. Others put their faith in Jesus on their deathbed at an old age, and others never get to know him.

I was thirty years old when I put my faith in Christ. I went to church as a kid but never understood any of it. God allows things to happen in our lives and does things to get our attention. But he can't make choices for us. We are in full control of our choices. That's why there are consequences for every choice you make. Only you can make that choice. You might have had a lot of influences, but you made the choice. We are born separated from God, following evil, and it is our choice to stop that by turning to Jesus Christ.

During the fourth plague, God made a distinction between the Egyptians and the Israelites. That would be his people and everybody else. The best way to put that is righteous and unrighteous. *Righteous* means "acting in accordance with divine or moral law." *Unrighteous* means "sinful, wicked, unjust, and unmerited." (Source: Merriam-Webster)

God makes a distinction between his people and everyone else. God loves everyone and wants everyone to know him, but there are consequences for every action and choice. Life will improve if you listen to God and do things his way. Things fall apart when we do things our way, just like they did for Egypt. When we are turned away from God, sin is in every area of our lives, and it feels like wrong choices cover us, just like the flies covered Egypt.

At some point in our lives, we get tired of how things are going and want to change. But we don't want to give up control. Flies ruled the pharaoh, and sin ruled Cain and caused him to kill his brother, but neither gave up their control. God didn't leave; he stayed with both of them, but they had to pay the consequences for their actions. What do you do?

The more we sin, the easier it becomes. The more you practice doing something, the easier it becomes to do. We want control and power over our lives. We focus more on getting what we want than gaining what we need. That's when everything we own becomes controlled by the sin in our life. We buy things to show our rebel-

CHOICES

lion, our sexuality, and the amount of money we have (high or low) to show we have control of our lives. Our lifestyle isn't to live comfortably. It's to show other people we have control of our lives. Some people want to show people they have some extra money, while others want to show people they don't care about money. Think about everything you own and how much you bought because you want others to see it. Even something as simple as a toothbrush. Someone may see it in your bathroom, so it has to look how you want it to because you have control of your life.

There is a big difference between getting what you want and having what you need. The Egyptians lost all their livestock, and they needed their animals, and the only thing they had to do was listen to God. Things would have begun to change if they had obeyed God. You will never feel satisfied when you focus on what you want, but you can feel completely content when you know you have and will continue to receive what you need.

During the fifth plague, all the livestock got sick and died. During the sixth plague, there were boils on every human. All the Egyptians had boils on their skin. That separated them from each other. Every disease, illness, disability, or other physical problems are because of the evil in this world. When we follow the path of evil in our lives, we physically separate ourselves from those who care about and love us. We surround ourselves with people who agree with the direction we are following. To put it another way, we surround ourselves with people with the same diseases. We are comfortable being around people who have the same illnesses we do. Whatever bad choices you make, you have that core group of "friends" making close to the same choices. At the same time, you push away the people who want to help. Then you tell your friends how stupid those people are, make more bad choices, and wish things would change. Whom do you listen to? Those who don't know what they should be doing? Those who care and want to help? Or God?

How do bad choices affect our lives? Like anything else, the more you do them, the more they affect you. Bad choices begin to destroy our lives. At first you don't notice what's happening, but then it becomes hail and demolishes everything. During the seventh plague, God sent hail and destroyed the majority of the land of Egypt. That is what sin does to us. Sin is just like frozen balls of water that strike your life. Imagine that, frozen chunks of water demolishing everything you own. Sin causes bad choices, bad choices cause our lives to fall apart, and then we gain anxiety, stress, and unrest. We are covered in sin, which is wrong choices. We focus on our possessions and how we look to others, whether in a good or bad way. Some of us enjoy looking bad to other people. And we are separated from those who honestly love us. Now our life is falling apart, filled with anxiety, stress, and unrest.

If you divide the word *disease*, it is *dis-ease* or *uneasiness*. You are already uneasy when separated from those who love and care about you. As life becomes more challenging, you begin to feel worse emotionally and mentally. Do you still want control of your life, or are you ready to try something different?

During the eighth plague, God sent locusts into Egypt, destroying any crops left after the hail. When you are filled with worry,

CHOICES

every moment of life is no longer a choice. You are just worrying about what will happen next. That is when you have lost all hope. No green grass is left, and you don't know where to turn, what to do, or whom to ask. You get to a point where there isn't anyone to turn to. Even your bad influences, your "friends", have other things to do. One person may still listen to you, but that's about it. You're numb to the world, filled with every type of worry, and you've forgotten what hope is. That's when everything goes pitch-black.

Like God says about the darkness in the ninth plague, you can feel that darkness. You barely have people around you, you don't know how to live, you have no hope, everything you say is a lie of some kind, and you are ready to give up. The last question you can ask yourself is, do you give up and die, or give up and start all over again? Death is the last step and the final plague. But understand that even if you get to complete darkness in life, you still have a choice.

The first plague is the Nile turning into blood. That means we still have blood in our veins but have lost our true strength and power, God. Now we are our own god. That is why life is so hard. We try and try and try, but we have no real strength or power.

The second plague is frogs. For us that means we are double-minded. It is almost impossible for us to focus on the best things for our lives. We always have at least two thoughts and choose which one to focus on.

The third plague is gnats or lice. For us that means the entire world that we live in is filled with evil. It's inside of us and all around us. We can't get away from it.

COMMANDMENTS

The fourth plague is flies. For us that is the beginning of darkness or evil taking over our lives. It begins to cover us and change us.

The fifth plague is death of the livestock. For us that is our possessions. We want money and power. Then we can do, say, and get whatever we want.

The sixth plague is boils. That is a physical, not spiritual, separation from people who want to help us have a better life.

The seventh plague is hail. For us this is our lives falling apart. We see the consequences of all our bad choices.

The eighth plague is locusts. For us this is the completion of our lives falling apart. We have nothing left, and our hope is gone.

The ninth plague is darkness. For us this is when we are ready to commit suicide. We see no future, have no hope, and are ready for it to end.

The tenth plague is the death of the firstborn son. For us this is death without knowing Jesus Christ. That is eternal separation from God in the pit of hell. The question is, how can we stop all this? How can we take back control of our lives so that evil won't rule over us?

We are going to look at the ten commandments. They are in the Bible in Exodus chapter 20.

The first commandment is, "You shall have no other gods before me." (Exo 20:3, NIV)

In other words, listen to God, and focus on him. If Adam and Eve had listened to God, they wouldn't have eaten the fruit. If the

CHOICES

pharaoh had listened to God, none of the plagues would have happened. If we would all listen to God, we would have a world filled with love, peace, and joy. If each one of us separately would listen to God, we wouldn't follow this path toward death. The first commandment fixes everything.

The second commandment is, "You shall not make for yourself a carved image, an idol, in the form of anything in the heavens above, the earth below, or the waters below the earth. You shall not bow down to them or worship them." (Exo 20:4-5a, NIV)

The Egyptians and other nations worshipped frogs. Every year when the Nile flooded, frogs would come out of it, showing that the land was fertile and ready to be planted. Anything to which we pay more attention than God becomes our god. Adam and Eve were focused more on their feeling of shame and knowledge of guilt than they were on God. Are you focused more on your feelings of shame and knowledge of guilt than on God? Think about all the things you have in your life that are harming you but still get more attention than God. These are things like smoking, overeating, watching TV, and drinking alcohol, soda, and other drinks with a lot of sugar. I could make a massive list of things we put before God, but these are examples. Think about how many things you do that are honestly killing you and you have difficulty stopping. Listen to God, put him first, and then you wouldn't be double-minded. You would be focused on spiritual things.

The third commandment is, "You shall not misuse the name of the Lord your God, for the Lord will not hold anyone guiltless who misuses his name." (Exo 20:7, NIV)

COMMANDMENTS

When the gnats or lice came from dust and went everywhere, the magicians said, "This is the finger of God." They admitted that God had done this and they couldn't do it. They respectfully used God's name. But the pharaoh still wouldn't listen to God.

The pharaoh broke the first three commandments by not listening to God when the magicians had told him this was the finger of God. The pharaoh didn't listen to God; he had other gods that had carved images; and now he had others telling him about God and didn't respect the name of God. Do you use the name of God to honor God? Or do you use his name when someone cuts you off in traffic or you hit your hand with a hammer? How many times a day do you misuse the name of the Lord?

The fourth commandment tells us to keep the Sabbath day holy. "You shall labor and do all your work in six days, but the seventh day is a sabbath to the Lord your God." (Exo 20:9-10a, NIV)

Sabbath means "to rest." (Source: Merriam-Webster)

God created everything in six days, and on the seventh day, he rested. We are supposed to follow that example. To keep it holy means to worship God. The seventh day is to be separated from every other day so we can rest and worship God. If we would worship God and focus on him, we wouldn't have the darkness beginning in our lives. If the pharaoh had worshipped God, turned to God, and become one of God's people, swarms of flies wouldn't have gone through the houses of the Egyptians. There were no flies in Goshen, the land of the Israelites, God's people. Do you ever take time to talk to God? Schedule a day and time, and set it aside just for him. It could be only ten minutes, but it's something. Now think about the things you schedule and make time for. How many of those things help you have a better life? I hope all of them, but we are better at making time for things that harm us than things that help us. We make time for everything except God.

The fifth commandment says, "Honor your mother and your father." (Exo 20:12a, NIV)

What that means is to listen to people that are older than you. Learn from their experiences, and you will have a better life. When you learn how to live from people older than you, they can teach you how to save money, use your time wisely, and care for yourself and your family. Everything falls apart when you learn to live independently and do things your way. During the fifth plague, the Egyptians lost all their livestock, but not a single one of the Israelites animals was touched. If we can learn that money, power, possessions, and control don't mean a thing, then we can learn how to have a good life.

I was about thirty years old when I had a rude awakening and said, "Oh no, everything she said was right." That's when I realized my mom was right and I was an idiot. My father passed away when I was eight. I understand what growing up without a dad is like. But when you turn to God, he will put the people in your life you need. You will always learn from personal experience, but taking what the older people around you tell you to heart will make a big difference. Learn from the wisdom of age.

The sixth commandment is, "You shall not murder." (Exo 20:13, NIV)

LIFE

To murder someone is to remove them from this life. You are judging someone physically. You decide your life is more important than theirs. Boils were the sixth plague, and they separated the Egyptians from each other just like sin separates us from those who love us. The pharaoh decided he was the judge, he was in control, and his life was more important than the Israelites. He wasn't allowing them to make sacrifices to God because he had the power and could do what he wanted. How many times do you blame your problems on other people? If they did things how you told them to, everything would be fine. But no, they have to do it how they want to. If all of us would listen to God and do things the way he tells us to, we wouldn't kill each other emotionally, spiritually, or physically.

The seventh commandment is, "You shall not commit adultery." (Exo 20:14, NIV)

That means the only time you have sex is when you are married and with someone of the opposite sex. I don't know if you agree with me, but I found in my own life that committing adultery was like having hail fall into every area of my life. When our wants and desires lead our life, our life will fall apart. Without God, we have no self-control and indulge in all kinds of crazy urges.

During the hailstorm, the seventh plague, the pharaoh admitted he had sinned. He said, "The Lord is right, and my people and I are wrong." He took back control as soon as the hail ended and wouldn't let the people go. When I read that, I wondered how stupid the pharaoh was. But then I realized I'd done this exact same thing in my life. I would have a physical relationship with a girl, realize what I was doing was wrong, end the relationship, and then find the next girl. You admit you're wrong, but nothing changes. How often have you felt like you were in the wrong or realized you were in the wrong, stopped what you were doing, and then did it somewhere else? If we could let go of our urges and follow our needs, things would change completely.

The eighth commandment is, "You shall not steal." (Exo 20:15, NIV)

When we steal, we take something that belongs to someone else. We need to understand how much our actions affect those around us. The locusts stole all the crops left after the hail in the eighth plague. The pharaoh was ready to let the people go, but then he asked who was going along. Moses said, "Everybody," and the pharaoh told him only the men could go. He stole hope from them. Which do you think is worse to lose—possessions and belongings, or hope and emotions? So how often do you steal hope and other emotions from the people around you? How many times do people steal them from you? How often do you wish people wouldn't steal them from you? How often do you think others wish you wouldn't steal those from them?

The ninth commandment is, "You shall not give false testimony against your neighbor." (Exo 20:16, NIV)

Or in other words, do not lie. People will stop trusting you when you say things about people who aren't true. People who don't trust you will start to separate themselves from you. You are all alone when you have no friends, family, coworkers, or even

COMMANDMENTS

enemies around you. That is when you can feel the darkness. That is when you hate yourself, everything you do, everywhere you go, and each thought you have, and you want it all to end. In the plague of darkness, the ninth plague, no one could see anyone else or move around. That is exactly how you feel when you get to that point. You feel stuck. You can't move out of this pit you're in, and everyone you see has a better life than you. At least that's how it feels. Now you have two choices: give up and die, or give up and live.

The tenth commandment is, "You shall not covet anything that belongs to your neighbor." (Exo20:17, NIV)

To covet means you want to possess or have something. (Source: Oxford languages)

Your neighbor has what they have, and you have what you have. It's very easy to look at other people's lives and see how much better their life is than yours. But they often look at your life and think it is better than theirs. We don't know everything that is going on in someone else's life. We can only see the top layer, and that always looks good. When you peel away the top layer and see the underneath parts, you see none of us has a perfect life. Many people who own a lot of things are in debt over their heads. Some people seem to have a fun life because they always have fun things to do. But in reality, they are so busy they barely have time to breathe and want to take a break. And you could easily break all the other commandments when you want what others have. Do you accept what God has given you, or do you want to be your own god and have power and control of your life? Do you want to be like the pharaoh or like Moses and Aaron? Or like Jesus Christ?

CHOICES

One day God will judge every single one of us. If we have broken even one of these commandments one time, we are guilty of sinning. If we sin, we will be separated from God for eternity. That means we won't be welcomed into heaven. Hell is the only place we can be if we are not in heaven. During the life that we live right now, we are separated from God, but he is still with us. If you think this life is horrible and honestly can't stand it, I highly recommend you get to know Jesus Christ because hell will be a thousand times, or more, worse than this, and it's for eternity, which means never-ending. Have you ever seen something burn or been on fire yourself? Imagine you continually felt the pain of that fire but never burned up and the fire never burned out. The feeling of acid melting your skin but it never ended. Your skin wouldn't melt, and you would continually feel the pain. Hell is for Satan and all his demons. God wants us to be in heaven with him. But how do we get there?

Many times, in different ways, the Bible says that we have all sinned. That is, every single human being that has or ever will live. We can't keep every one of the ten commandments. When our conscious mind fully develops, and we can understand good and evil, we sin. As soon as the Israelites became free from the Egyptians, they began to sin. God gave them many laws and rules. They had to sacrifice certain animals for specific reasons. Animals' blood is pure. Animals can't sin. Animals live by instinct, not by thought and reason. You need innocent blood to cover your tainted, sinful blood. The only man who never sinned was Jesus Christ. He died on the cross, and his pure blood covers all our sins as long as we believe he died for us and that he is God.

COMMANDMENTS

The ten plagues are the walk of death for us. If we follow the path of the plagues, we will experience death. Physical death is your body going into the ground. But we have a soul, which is our inner being, and a spirit that connects us to God. Both of those go into the afterlife when our body dies. We need to know how we are given eternal life. We cannot earn eternal life. We need to walk through the gates and be given a brand-new life. Come along, and follow me through the gates.

Gates

When God freed the Israelites from Egypt, they no longer had people controlling them. They were no longer slaves. They could do whatever they wanted, how they wanted, and when they wanted. They were like teenagers with a brand-new, or most likely slightly used, car. They had something none of them had ever experienced—freedom. Now they had the opportunity to better their lives as well as the lives of those around them. And they knew God was with them. God was the one who set them free. God was about to give them a brand-new life in a brand-new land, and God would lead and guide them through Moses. The only thing the Israelites needed to do was trust and obey God.

The question is, now what? The Israelites were in the wilderness with nothing. The only supplies they had were what they had taken from Egypt. But God was giving them what they needed. He gave them manna from heaven. Manna is like bread. It tasted like wafers made with honey, and it would fall from the sky like dew every morning. God told them they should only take what they

CHOICES

needed for one day, except the day before the Sabbath. On that day, they should take enough for two days. Also, God was a cloud during the day and fire at night that they could follow. God did many things for them and gave many things to them, but they still complained. They said, "Why did you bring us out of Egypt to kill us with thirst?" Then God gave them water from a rock. The Israelites were looking back at their life in Egypt. They remembered the good things but ignored the abuse that went along with it. Now they were free, no more abuse, but they still didn't have everything they wanted. God gave them what they needed. God had to teach them how to live this new life of freedom. They wandered around in the wilderness for forty years.

After those forty years, God brought them into the land he had promised to Abraham: the land of Canaan. That land would become Jerusalem. Many, many things happened and continue to happen in Jerusalem. There is only one thing I want to focus on, and that is the rebuilding of the wall. That event is in the book of Nehemiah. It starts in Nehemiah chapter 3. But before that, in 2 Kings 25, the Bible tells us about the Babylonian army marching into Jerusalem. They set fire to the temple, the royal palace, and all the houses in Jerusalem. They broke down the walls around Jerusalem, and anyone who survived the attack they took back to Babylon. The Israelites were in Babylon for about seventy years.

At the beginning of Nehemiah, a few men came to talk to Nehemiah, and he questioned them. He asked them about the Jewish people who survived the time in Babylon and about Jerusalem. The men told Nehemiah that those who survived the time in Babylon were back in Jerusalem. But they were in great trouble and disgraced. The wall around Jerusalem was broken down and all its gates burned. Nehemiah mourned and prayed for some days. God told Nehemiah to rebuild the wall around Jerusalem. They would need to rebuild the wall first to rebuild the city of Jerusalem. The wall was their protection.

The wall had towers that would help protect the city and gates that would lead to different areas of the city. There were ten gates in the wall they rebuilt. The first gate was the Sheep Gate, then the Fish Gate, the Old Gate, the Valley Gate, the Dung Gate, the Fountain Gate, the Water Gate, the Horse Gate, the East Gate, and the Inspection Gate. The Israelites, or Jewish people, all worked together and rebuilt the wall in fifty-two days. Amazing things happen when we unite, especially when we unite with God. (Source: vocabulary.com)

The first gate is the Sheep Gate. The high priest and his brothers or fellow priests rebuilt the Sheep Gate. They rebuilt the Sheep Gate, consecrated it, and hung its doors. When something is consecrated, it is dedicated to a higher purpose and made holy. (Source: vocabulary.com, Neh 3:1a, NIV)

To be holy is to be set apart, to be devoted entirely to God. (Source: Firm, Fellowship of Israel related ministries)

They would bring sheep through this gate to be sacrificed. First, they might wash them in the pool of Bethesda because that was close to the Sheep Gate. The sheep would be brought into the city and taken to the temple. Outside the temple was the altar, which was used to offer animals to God. The sheep were sacrificed to cover the sins of the people. I want you to fully understand that no animal was ever sacrificed to God to please him. One more time,

CHOICES

God was already pleased. He just wanted people to be closer to him. They could only be closer to him if their sins were covered by innocent blood.

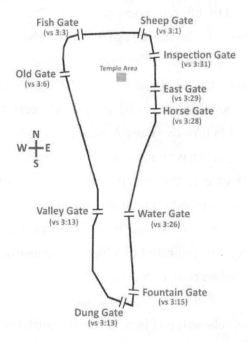

(Source: https://jesusplusnothing.com/series/post/nehem3)

When they brought sheep through the Sheep Gate, which was consecrated, the sheep became perfect. Animals can't sin because they don't have a conscious mind. They don't reason things out, so they don't actually make choices. They live by natural instinct.

They have evil inside them, which causes them to do evil things. But since they aren't making a choice, it isn't sinning. Sheep became completely perfect after an Israelite walked the sheep through that gate. When someone offers them to God by sacrificing them, the innocent blood covered their sin. Then they became innocent or sinless and closer to God. The high priest at that time was Eliashib. *Eliashib* means "God restores" or "God of conversion." (Source: Bible study tools and She knows)

That would happen when a sheep or lamb's blood covered a Jewish person's sins. God would restore them and begin to change or convert them. The priests consecrated the wall around Jerusalem from the Sheep Gate to the Tower of the Hundred and the Tower of Hananel. The priests rebuilt both towers, protecting the wall's north part.

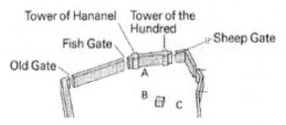

(Source: https://scripture-for-today.blogspot.com/2011/12/nehemiah-3-built-repaired-and-restored.html)

The second gate is the Fish Gate. The sons of Hassenaah rebuilt the Fish Gate. They laid its beams and set its doors, bolts, and bars. *Hassenaah* means "thorny." (Source: Truth Unity, Neh 3:3-4, NIV)

CHOICES

When something is thorny, there is work involved. It isn't just given to you; you must work for it. When Adam and Eve were in the Garden of Eden, they didn't have to work for their food. God gave it to them. The trees and plants grew fruits and vegetables without being planted or working the soil. After they sinned, God cursed the ground, and the plants grew thorns and thistles. Adam and Eve had to work the ground to eat from the plants in the field. The Fish Gate is where the fish market was, and it led out of the city toward the northwest. Fishermen would bring catches and sell them by salting or drying them. Being on the north wall, it was the closest to the Lake of Galilee. It was convenient for those bringing fish from the Jordan or most parts of the Mediterranean coast. Many merchants would locate closer to the northern gates than any other because they would get most of their business from the northern gates. That is because the north side was the best way to enter Jerusalem. The northern side was mainly on a plain, while the other sides of the city overlooked steep ravines. Because the fishermen wanted to make money, they would violate the Sabbath by selling fish that day. The Sabbath was a day of rest dedicated to God. That was the day you stopped working and worshipped God.

The third gate in the wall was the Old Gate. The Old Gate was repaired and strengthened by Joiada and Meshullan. They laid its beams and set its doors, bolts, and bars. (Neh 3:6)

The Babylonians only partially destroyed the Old Gate. The men had to repair parts of the Old Gate and strengthen other parts of it. Unlike the Sheep Gate and the Fish Gate, there wasn't a specific use for the Old Gate. It was a place where the city's elders would meet to discuss matters of community importance and issue judgment on disputes.

Hanun and the people of Zanoah repaired the Valley Gate, the fourth gate. They rebuilt it; set its doors, bolts, and bars; and fixed 1,500 feet of the wall as far as the Dung Gate. The Valley Gate led to the Hinnom Valley. In that valley, horrible things happened during the history of Jerusalem. The Israelites worshipped other gods and sacrificed children by fire to those gods. The valley was considered ceremonially unclean, and human bones were spread over it. Then it became a place for garbage dumping and burning corpses of criminals and animals. It became used as a symbol of hell. Its name changed to *Gehinnom* or *Gehanna*, which means "hell." (Source: Wiktionary, Neh 3:13, NIV)

It isn't a place people would want to visit. The people that fixed the Valley Gate worked there until they finished the repairs of the gate and wall. That would've been challenging.

The next gate was the Dung Gate. You can imagine what the Jewish people used the Dung Gate for. They took all the refuse and dung out through it. It led to the Valley of Gehanna, or "hell," where they burnt all the trash. Malchijah repaired the fifth gate, which was the Dung Gate. He rebuilt it and set its doors, bolts, and bars. Malchijah was the ruler of Beth Hakkerem, and *Beth Hakkerem* means "house of the vineyard." (Source: Wikipedia, Neh 3:14, NIV)

It was a city where they planted grapevines and made wine. *Rechab*, the name of his father, means "driver and controller." (Source: Truth Unity)

CHOICES

That is a picture of self-control, not giving in to your desires and urges. The Rechabites, descendants of Rechab, were separatists who refused to participate in agricultural pursuits or drink wine. Believing that the seminomadic way of life was a religious obligation, they herded their flocks over much of Israel and Judah. Malchijah was the ruler of a people who planted vineyards and made wine. At the same time, his father and his descendants believed you shouldn't sow seeds, drink wine, or build houses but keep moving to where the grass is greener. Malchijah was much different than his father and his people.

Shallum, son of Col-hozeh, ruler of the district of Mizpah, repaired the Fountain Gate, the sixth gate. He built it, covered it, and set its doors, bolts, and bars. He also built the wall of the Pool of Shelah of the king's garden, as far as the stairs that went down to the city of David. The Fountain Gate led to the Gihon Spring, Jerusalem's sole perennial water source. That water wouldn't have stood still. (Neh 3:15, NIV)

The seventh gate is the Water Gate. No one made repairs to the Water Gate. Or at least it's not mentioned in the scripture, which is different from every other gate. There were no great rivers near Jerusalem, and the city depended on reservoirs and springs for its water. The Water Gate was used to bring water into the city and the temple for festivals and celebrations.

The next gate, the eighth gate, was the Horse Gate. The priests repaired the Horse Gate, close to the king's stables and the temple. That would have been a beautiful gateway. The men of Jerusalem would ride their horses out of that gate to war. After the war, the king's chariots would pass through the gates triumphantly on their way back into the city. Horses became a symbol of war. (Neh 3:28, NIV)

After them, Shemaiah, the keeper of the East Gate, made repairs. The East Gate led right up to the temple and was the ninth gate. (Neh 3:29b, NIV)

A goldsmith repaired the wall as far as the house of the temple servants and the merchants. He also repaired the Inspection Gate, the tenth gate, and up to the upper house of the corner. Goldsmiths and merchants repaired between the upper house of the corner and the Sheep Gate. The Israelites assembled at the Inspection Gate for various purposes—things like judging, legal transactions, giving instructions, and preparing for battle. (Neh 3:31-32, NIV)

That is every gate in the wall around Jerusalem. Now we need to get a complete understanding of what all these gates represent.

The Sheep Gate is Jesus Christ. When we put our faith in or walk into Jesus, we are like a sheep or lamb walking through the Sheep Gate. We are made perfect and holy, or in other words, consecrated and set apart. That's why the priests rebuilt that gate. In the Old Testament, priests were the connection between man and God. But now Jesus is our connection to God. As soon as you accept Christ as your Savior, you can communicate directly with God. When the priests built the Sheep Gate, they consecrated it before they finished working on it. Understand that we don't have to do any work to put our faith in Jesus. We need to believe and take that step. Then we are covered by the blood of Jesus, the perfect Lamb of God. We are covered by the blood of Christ, forgiven for every single

CHOICES

one of our sins—past and future—and have direct communication with God. When we sin, God sees the blood of Christ covering us, and he sees us as pure white, innocent, and perfect.

The name of the high priest was Eliashib. His name means "restoring and converting," which is exactly what God does for us. God restores us to himself and changes us from the inside out. We take one step, and God begins to repair us. God gives us his grace, speaks to us, and now we can talk to him. We are given these gifts for free. God does the work, hangs the doors, and we just step through the gate and put our faith in Christ. If we decide to walk out of the Sheep Gate, we take back control of our lives. We gave God control when we walked into the Sheep Gate. But now we are stepping back into the wilderness, and God has to try to get our attention again, which could be in many different ways. God wouldn't even try to get your attention if he didn't love you.

```
Fish Gate                        Sheep Gate
(vs 3:3)                         (vs 3:1)
```

When we walk through the Fish Gate, we become a disciple of Jesus. When Jesus started his ministry, the first men he called were fishermen. Jesus called twelve disciples and told them, "Follow me, and I will make you fishers of men." (Mat 4:19, NIV)

That means that Jesus will give us the tools and abilities we need, but we must do the work. We need to lay the beams and set the doors, bolts, and bars. We need to share our testimonies, our stories, with others—that is, telling people what God has done for us after we put our faith in Christ.

When we accept Christ as our Savior, life becomes exciting, and we want everyone to know about it, like a child with a new toy. A child wants everyone to see their toy because, to them, it's the greatest thing they have ever experienced. Jesus is the greatest thing you can experience. The hard part about sharing him with others is that everything is happening inside you. You can't show Jesus to people. You can only tell them about him and what he is doing in your life. But you need to throw your story out among your friends, family, coworkers, and people you just met to see who will bite. Who will take an interest in what you're saying? You are not a salesman trying to get people to buy a new product. You are a child of God that wants others to meet their true father. If you walk out of the Fish Gate, you will still have faith, but you won't have any actions to go with it. When the Bible says, "Lay the beams and set the doors, bolts, and bars," it means there is work we, as Christians, have to do.

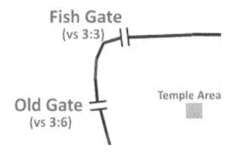

CHOICES

The Old Gate is where we learn God's old ways. You give up your old self and way of life and learn to live by God's wisdom. The picture shows that we go around a corner here and start to head south. God begins to take us through a humbling process. In our world, 99 percent of the things we know are lies. Now we need to learn the truth straight from the mouth of God. We need to study his Word, the Bible, go to church, interact with other Christians, have Bible studies, and do whatever will help us learn how to live a new and better life. The truth will give you a much better life. You can only gain wisdom from God. God provides us with the truth and a brand-new understanding of everything.

God's ways never change. God has always been the same. We are the ones that change. We can barely decide what to eat for dinner because we might miss out on something better. Walking into the Old Gate is letting go of your old ways and following God's teachings. In the Bible, Ephesians 4:22 says, "You were taught, with regard to your former way of life, to put off your old self, which is being corrupted by its deceitful desires, to be made new in the attitude of your minds, and to put on the new self, created to be like God in true righteousness and holiness." (Version NIV)

If you walk out of the Old Gate, you will look for the newest teachings and follow them. There is always a new religious trend to follow. If you give up on God's truth, you will follow whatever the most contemporary "truth" is that sounds good to you.

Next is the Valley Gate. In the Valley Gate, we learn through trials. The picture has three corners, and the last is the sharpest.

GATES

There are three events we go through during the Valley Gate. The last one is the hardest. During these trying times, we are humbled and taught how to survive. It's great to have knowledge and understanding, but if we never use it, how does it help us? During our Valley Gate experience, God will teach us how to use the wisdom we gained during our Old Gate experience. That is a very trying time. We experience hardships, and we struggle with doubts. We learn how weak we honestly are and how much we need God. You learn how disgusting, filthy, self-centered, and horrible you are. Like any other muscle, the more you use it, the stronger it becomes.

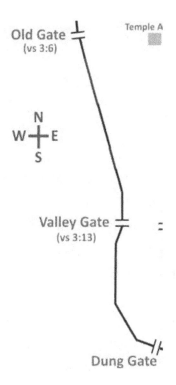

CHOICES

We must go through these trials and temptations to grow our faith and eliminate our fleshly desires. In the Old Testament, God would sometimes appear as fire. Think of this time as God burning off your fleshly desires so that you will lean on him and follow his ways. Nothing beautiful can grow on a mountaintop, but valleys are filled with beauty and richness. God will take you off your mountaintop, humble you, and make you spiritually beautiful and rich through trials. If you walk out of the Valley Gate, you are giving up and not learning or growing. You have the wisdom God gave you but aren't using it, and you give up during those trying times.

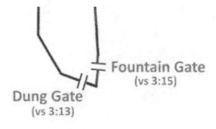

When you step through the Dung Gate, a lot of the junk, or dung, comes out of your life. Your Valley Gate experience can go on for a while. It depends on how much you learn and grow. But that has nothing to do with being a fast learner or a good Christian. God knows when the time is right and you are ready to move on. You will clearly see the results of the Valley Gate when you walk through the Dung Gate. The Valley Gate experience prepares you for the Dung Gate. There will be a point in your life when something happens that will start the removal of your most significant weaknesses. I almost died at that point. I felt my spirit beginning to leave my body, and I prayed, screamed, and cried. That was the craziest night I have had at this point in my life. That was when I walked through the Dung Gate. I took that experience as a warning from God that if I continued to live like I was, I would die. Then I noticed God giving me other warnings. Those warnings made me do a lot of thinking and praying. I paid more attention to my choices and depended more on God. Then God began removing my most significant issues. None of that is easy, but all of it is worth it. The best way to refine something is by fire. Walking through fire is what we must go through to experience a better life. If you walk out of the Dung Gate, any junk removed from your life will return, and the rest will stay.

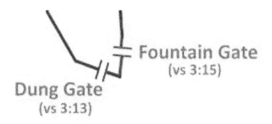

Next, we walk through the Fountain Gate. Somewhere between the Dung Gate and the Fountain Gate, there's a moment when you can no longer walk out of the gates. You can't turn around and move backward. You can only move forward. I believe it happens at that very sharp corner in the picture. That isn't a fact, just a thought. But notice that you start to move north. When we choose to step through the Fountain Gate, life will change forever. We are cleansed and empowered by the Holy Spirit for our Christian walk. The Holy Spirit is flowing through us like a fountain. The moment we put our faith in Christ, we receive the Holy Spirit. The Holy Spirit is our direct communication with God. Also, that's how God communicates with us. When God removes the junk, the dung, from our lives, there is more room for the Holy Spirit to work in and through us. Now our only goal and desire is to do the will of God. We are still human, and we will make mistakes, but God and his plans are what we stay focused on.

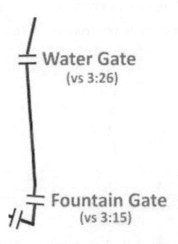

Next is the Water Gate. We don't step into the Water Gate. As I mentioned above, no one had to repair the Water Gate, and the scriptures only mention the Water Gate. Every other gate needed to be repaired by someone, just like we need to do some work in our broken lives and then choose to walk through the gate. The act of

GATES

walking through a gate gives that problem to God. We admit we are wrong and ask God for help, and he fixes it. When we walk through the Fountain Gate, the Holy Spirit is flowing through us. Then God moves us into the Water Gate when we are ready. At that point, the Holy Spirit isn't only flowing through us but is leading our lives. No longer are we trying to decide what steps we should take, but the Holy Spirit leads us to where we need to go. We can still get off track and take the wrong steps, but we turn to God, ask for help, and he puts us where we need to be.

Life is more like a path we are following: we may take a step off that path, but nothing major happens. Then we admit we need help, ask God for help, and he helps us. Early in our Christian walk, it's more like we are a train on tracks, and every wrong step is our life derailing. Then we have to do a lot of work to return to where we had been. But now we are following the Holy Spirit. The Holy Spirit leads our life, and life is much simpler. There will always be struggles and trials. They're just a part of life. Also notice how much straighter the shape of Jerusalem is on this side. The path of life is much smoother.

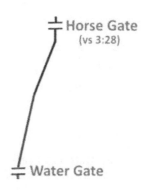

CHOICES

The next gate is the Horse Gate. The priests repaired this gate. The reason is that the Horse Gate is spiritual warfare. Our warfare with Satan and his demons will increase as we grow closer to God. But now we have the weapons, wisdom, and faith we need to overcome these battles. Satan wants to pull us away from God. Satan doesn't care if we follow him. He doesn't want us to live the life God has planned for us. Satan hates us. He is pure evil and will do whatever he can to keep us from having a relationship with God. But at this point in our walk with Christ, there's nothing Satan can do to take us away from God. We have already won this war through what Christ did and our faith in him. God, Jesus, and the Holy Spirit have given us many weapons which we need to use. We must continue to remind Satan that we have all the authority and he has none. Never give in to Satan, and always fight back.

```
—— East Gate                          —— Inspection Gate
   (vs 3:29)      Temple Area            (vs 3:31)
—— Horse Gate
   (vs 3:28)                          —— East Gate
                                         (vs 3:29)
```

The East Gate is next, and that is the return of Christ. One day Jesus will return to the earth and gather all the believers.

Next to the East Gate is the Inspection Gate. The Inspection Gate is judgment day, also known as the final judgment. Every single one of us—that is, every person that has ever had the breath of life in them—all of us will stand before the throne of God and have to answer for everything we have done in this life. If God has your name written in the Book of Life, you will spend eternity with God in heaven. If your name is not in the Book of Life, you will spend eternity in hell, suffering forever.

Please understand that *eternity* means "forever," never-ending, and after we die or Jesus comes back, there are no second chances. (Source: Vocabulary.com)

You cannot earn your way into heaven. It doesn't matter how much good you have done in your life. That does not get you into heaven. Even if you only sin one time, you will go to hell. Doing good doesn't cover your sin. Only the blood of Jesus Christ covers your sin. If God hasn't forgiven your sin because you haven't accepted Jesus as your Lord and Savior, you will not go to heaven.

These are our steps to eternal life. Each gate is a step closer to God. God will give us a new and better life. Life is a struggle because we are in a spiritual battle. Our choices are to ignore the spiritual warfare and try to get by, live like we are already dead by following the evil, or put our faith in Jesus Christ. Then we see life in a completely different way and start to live.

These are the steps to life. First, put your faith in Christ, and give your life to God. Then follow him by becoming his disciple and bring others to Christ by sharing your testimony. After that, learn God's old ways and follow God's true teachings. Then you will learn through trials, which will refine you, so God can remove all that junk from your life. Then you will be cleansed and empowered by the Holy Spirit. After that, the Holy Spirit makes God's Word come alive in our lives, and the Holy Spirit will lead us. Then we experience spiritual warfare because of how close we have become to God. All these steps are our personal experiences. The following two steps are for all of humanity. They are the return of Christ and then the final judgment.

Death is our body entering the ground and our soul and spirit entering the afterlife. I think of this life as a preseason game. Most sports have games that prepare them for the season. Usually, the preseason only lasts a few months, but the season is much longer than that. If a player plays their position well enough, the coach will use them during the season. Our coach is Jesus. He is also our biggest fan. He cheers us on and teaches us how to live. Life is our preseason, and if we continue to have faith, we will enjoy complete bliss in heaven for the rest of the season, which is eternity.

What does this have to do with what we have been discussing? What does this have to do with the Nile turning blood? That was the first plague, and Egypt lost its power and strength when it didn't have the water of the Nile. The same thing happened to Adam and Eve when they sinned. They lost their power and strength, which was God.

The first commandment is, "You shall have no other gods before me." (Exo 20:3, NIV)

Egypt had many other gods, and when God spoke to the pharaoh, he didn't listen. Adam and Eve only knew the one true

God, but they didn't listen to him when Satan spoke. The one thing they needed to do was listen to God, but they didn't.

That's where we are today. To be able to put God first in our lives, we have to put our faith in Jesus Christ. Then his blood will cover our lives, and we will be restored to God and have his power and strength in our lives. Christ's blood will be everywhere in our lives. We will enter our new city and start a relationship with God, giving us his strength and power. Now it's time to put all this together and properly understand it. Move out of your life as a slave and enter into the land God has waiting just for you.

The Ten Tens

In the third chapter of Genesis, Adam chose to take the fruit that Eve offered him, and he ate it. That was fruit from the tree God told them not to eat from, the Tree of the Knowledge of Good and Evil. Eve was lied to by Satan and gave into his temptation. Adam saw what happened to Eve and still chose to eat the fruit. Adam wasn't lied to or tempted by Satan. He decided to eat the fruit of his own free will. That's why Adam committed the first sin. He chose to sin. Eve thought what she was doing was the right thing to do. Satan tricked Eve into sinning. Humanity is separated from God because Adam made one choice to disobey God. Because of the evil inside of us, we can't be in God's perfect and holy presence. If we saw God's face, we would die. That means we are born into a world ruled by evil and separated from our creator, who loves us. God has full control of both heaven and earth. Satan rules over the earth, but he doesn't control anything. Satan lies to us, tempts us, manipulates us, and tricks us. Then we give him control of our lives, and he rules over us. That is why we need Christ in our lives. Christ reconnects us to God.

CHOICES

We sin constantly. We are continually disobeying God. We all deserve to be cast into hell, the lake of fire. But Christ took our place. He took the penalty we deserve. God wants us to be with him for eternity, but Satan wants to separate us from God for eternity. Where we end up is our choice. We are in a spiritual battle, but God has given us all the weapons we need to get through it, and Jesus has already won. Our fight is against death, and Jesus overcame death. Ephesians 6:12 says, "Our struggle is not against flesh and blood, but against the rulers, against the authorities, against the powers of this dark world and against the spiritual forces of evil in the heavenly realms." (Version NIV)

Our fight isn't against other humans. It is against Satan, demons, and all other evil spirits. The next verse, Ephesians 6:13, talks about the whole armor of God, which is what we need to put on to overcome all of these evil things.

The first plague was the Nile River turning into blood. That caused the Egyptians to lose their power source, which gave them strength. God separated Adam and Eve from himself when they sinned, causing them to lose their power source and strength. God was their power source, and he gave them strength. We are innocent, not guilty of any sin until we are between the ages of eleven and thirteen. That's when our conscious mind fully develops, and we can understand how to make choices for ourselves.

The first commandment is, "Have no other gods before me." (Exo 20:3, NIV)

If God were always the most important thing in our lives, we would always have strength, guidance, and protection. But Satan constantly tempts us to do evil, and because we are weak, we give in to those temptations. That's why we need to walk through the Sheep Gate. We need to have faith in Christ. Christ reconnects us to God. Then God puts his Spirit inside of us. That is the Holy Spirit. The moment we step through the Sheep Gate, put our faith in Jesus, we receive the Holy Spirit. We literally have a piece of God inside of us. Now we have the ability to talk directly to God. We don't need to pray to anyone else or through anyone else. We pray straight to God in the name or character of Jesus.

When we end a prayer by saying "in Jesus's name," we're saying we have covered our old way of living with the way Christ lives and use the power of his name to request the answering of our prayers. We're no longer living by our will but through the blood of Christ. There is no reason for us to pray to Jesus's mother, Mary. She is not God. She gave birth to God, and God used her as an amazing tool, but she is a human, just like the rest of us. There is nowhere in the Bible that it mentions praying to or through Mary. Every person who has accepted Jesus Christ as their Lord and Savior is completely reconnected to God and can talk directly to him, as a friend speaks to a friend.

Frogs came out of the Nile during the second plague and went everywhere in Egypt. Frogs went into the pharaoh's palace, into his bedroom, onto his bed, into the houses of his officials, onto the Egyptians, and into their ovens and kneading bowls. Frogs covered the land.

The second commandment says, "You shall have no idols." (Exo 20:4, NIV)

CHOICES

You are just like those frogs when you follow whoever or whatever you want to. You're hopping from one place to the next, wandering all over the land, living in the water for a little, living on the land for a while, but having no real direction. You don't have any guidance. You might have plans and goals but don't know how to achieve them. You keep trying and hope something will work out in your favor. When you walk through the Fish Gate, you're choosing to become a disciple of Jesus. You are choosing to follow him. You are no longer a frog who lives on land or in water, but now you're a fish who can only survive in water.

When you become a disciple of Jesus, you follow him. You have the Holy Spirit inside you, guiding and directing you while God teaches you. Jesus says, in John 7:38, "Whoever believes in me streams of living water will flow through him." And verse 39 says, "Now this he (Jesus) said about the Holy Spirit."

The Holy Spirit is compared to water often in the Bible. You are living in the guidance of the Holy Spirit, swimming in the stream God created just for you. God has a plan for you. God made a plan for your life before you were born, and now you need to stay focused on him and move with God's current.

In the third plague, all the dust in Egypt turned into small insects and covered every human and animal. Evil spread everywhere when God banished Adam and Eve from the Garden of Eden. Evil spread to every human and animal. And it's been that way to this very day. Evil is everywhere, in us and all around us.

The third commandment says, "Do not take the Lord's name in vain or misuse the name of the Lord." (Exo 20:7, NIV)

Only evil can speak negatively against God. We need to learn from God's old ways and stop learning from the practices of this world. We need to walk through the Old Gate. We need to learn straight from the mouth of God. Our world is Satan's domain, and he spreads lies upon lies upon lies. None of us knows anything. Throughout our whole lives, many different sources teach us many different lies. But Satan's behind all of them.

Through our direct connection to God, he will give us new wisdom. But we need to do our part and press into God. We need to read the Bible and have others explain the things we don't understand. The closer we want to get to God, the more Satan will attack us. We need to pray to God and ask for help continually. Talk to God like he is your friend. Talk to him over coffee, through tears, on your knees, while driving, or doing whatever you do. God hears you, loves hearing from you, and is always there for you. Never feel like he is too busy for you. He loves you. Learn God's ways, and ask him to eliminate your ways.

During the fourth plague, swarms of flies ruined the land of Egypt. But God didn't send a single fly to the land of the Israelites, Goshen. God made a distinction between his people and the Egyptians. God did the same thing with Cain and Abel. Abel offered him fat portions, which he accepted, but Cain offered him fruits of the soil, which God didn't accept. God accepts what is righteous but will not accept what is unrighteous. The Egyptians didn't worship God, but the Israelites did.

The fourth commandment is, "Keep the Sabbath day Holy." (Exo 20:8, NIV)

CHOICES

On the Sabbath, you stopped all your work and praised God. On the Sabbath, you would be made spiritually clean and separate yourself from this world and its uncleanliness. Flies are dirty, annoying, frustrating, and distracting. Sin is uncleanliness. It confuses us and distracts us from doing God's will. When we step into the Valley Gate, God begins to prepare us. God wants to remove the sin in our lives, but we need to be in the right place spiritually.

When times are hard, you want to rest. When you feel dirty, you want to be clean. When you see God moving in your life, you want to praise and worship him. If you only focus on your struggles, the swarms of flies will never leave, but if you continue to rely on God and pray to him, he will remove them. Walking through the Valley Gate is hard, but it's worth it. Give yourself to God and allow him to refine you.

The Egyptians lost all their livestock during the fifth plague. But this is when God blessed Adam and Eve with another son, Seth. God blesses those who follow him.

The fifth commandment is, "Honor your father and your mother." (Exo 20:12a, NIV)

You need to learn from people older than you are. They have had more experiences and can help us have a better life. Do we try to get what we want or search for what we need? Getting what we want doesn't satisfy us. It only quenches our thirst. Getting what we need isn't always what we want, but it will satisfy us. When you feel satisfied, you begin to feel content with life, and life becomes much better. Then we walk through the Dung Gate, and God removes our desire for power, money, and control. God takes away the sin in our lives. We will still make mistakes, but much less than we used to. Remember, God is the one who removes sin from your life. You are following him and doing his work, but God is transforming you. You are still you, and you always will be you. God is sanding down your rough edges.

During the sixth plague, the Egyptians had boils all over their bodies. In Genesis 6:3, God judged humanity physically and made our life span no longer than 120 years.

The sixth commandment is, "Do not murder." (Exo 20:13, NIV)

When we intentionally kill someone, we judge them. We are separating them from everyone who cares about them, saying, "I'm right, and you're wrong," and harming them physically, spiritually, and emotionally. The Holy Spirit fills us and our life when we walk through the Fountain Gate. Then we begin to see everyone differently and genuinely care about everyone. When the Holy Spirit is flowing through you, love becomes real. For the first time, you begin to love people. You want to help people. Only evil wants to destroy people's lives. God loves us and softens our hearts through the Holy Spirit. Then we care about others and are willing to help them put their lives back together. Sadly, evil will always be inside of us, and we will always have evil thoughts. But our actions show our hearts. When our hearts are softened, we will help others and do whatever we can not to harm anyone.

The seventh plague was hail. Hail causes a lot of damage. When things fall into your life that cause a lot of damage, you gain anxiety, stress, and unrest.

CHOICES

The seventh commandment is, "Do not commit adultery." (Exo 20:14, NIV)

Usually, sexual sins cause the most damage in our lives. That could be thinking about sex, pornography, sex without marriage, incest, rape, etc. Adultery always affects at least two people. If you see someone and fantasize about them, you see them as a sex object. Then you will treat that person as a sex object. If you look at pornography, you are indulging in the pain of someone else's life. You are negatively affecting their life. When you enter the Water Gate, the Holy Spirit begins to lead your life. All the hail melts, and now you have peace, calmness, and rest. The Holy Spirit leads you on the exact path you need to be on, and you simply follow. You feel content with life, and that is the best feeling you can have. Remember, hail is solid pieces of ice falling from the sky, destroying everything it touches. The Holy Spirit is like hail that melted since he is often compared to water. The Holy Spirit doesn't fall on you. He comes from inside you, and he helps you. He doesn't lead you into things you're not ready to experience. He shows you the way that is the best way for you.

The eighth plague was locusts. The locusts stole whatever crops the Egyptians had left after the hail. They ate them all. When tough times fall into your life, you begin to lose hope. You have no hope left when things completely fall apart, and you lose your mind.

The eighth commandment is, "Do not steal." (Exo 20:15, NIV)

You can steal things from people that cause emotional, spiritual, and physical pain. Something like kidnapping, stealing someone's child, affects people in all three ways. Physically, they can't hug their child. Emotionally, they are mourning, worried, stressed, and experiencing a thousand other feelings. Spiritually, they may doubt God. We are going into spiritual warfare when we step through the Horse Gate. Satan has been stealing our lives from us long enough, and now God gives us every tool we need to fight back. But God does the fighting. He protects us. We just need to ask. God fights for us and for the people around us. The worst thing Satan can steal from us is our relationship with Jesus Christ. When we choose to have a relationship with Jesus Christ, no one, not even Satan himself, can take that from us. We need to choose a relationship with Jesus and keep moving forward through the gates of life. Do not steal anything from anyone, but help them have a new life.

A darkness the Egyptians could feel came during the ninth plague. It was so dark the Egyptians couldn't move around. They couldn't see, so they couldn't go anywhere or do anything.

The ninth commandment is, "Do not lie." (Exo 20:16, NIV)

When you lie, people will stop trusting you, give up on you, and walk out of your life. When you have no hope and no friends and are left with only confusion, you have no life. You can feel darkness when you don't want to go anywhere or see anyone and wish you were dead. Jesus is the light, and the ninth gate is the East Gate, which is the return of Jesus. Someday soon, Jesus will return and gather his followers. Jesus will take Christians to heaven, and everyone else will experience the tribulations. You don't want to be on earth during the tribulations.

The last plague, the tenth, was the death of the firstborn. Every firstborn son in Egypt died.

CHOICES

The tenth commandment is, "Do not covet." (Exo20:17, NIV)

When you want what someone else has, you could easily break every other commandment. But if you break only one commandment one time, you have sinned. One sin equals eternity in hell. The tenth gate is the Inspection Gate. The Inspection Gate is the final judgment. You will stand before God and answer for everything you did throughout your entire life. If you have faith in Christ, God has forgiven you for every sin you ever committed, and Jesus will welcome you into eternal bliss. If you never got to know Jesus, God will punish you for your sins in the lake of fire.

Where are you? Are you experiencing the plagues and on the path of death, or do you have faith in Christ while you walk through the gates of life? The most important thing to understand and know is where you are in life. Are you fully alive or living half dead? Do you believe in some higher power or give thanks to the man upstairs? Neither one of those is God. They are man-made ideas of God. The Trinity is God, Jesus Christ, and the Holy Spirit. They are not three separate beings. They are three parts of one God. If you can't say "Thank you, God" and mean it, evil has consumed you.

Plague	Commandment	Gate
Nile to Blood	Have no other gods before me.	Sheep Gate
Frogs	Have no idols.	Fish Gate
Dust to gnats	Do not take the Lord's name in vain.	Old Gate
Flies	Keep the Sabbath.	Valley Gate
Livestock	Honor your mother and father.	Dung Gate
Boils	Do not murder.	Fountain Gate

THE TEN TENS

Hail	Do not commit adultery.	Water Gate
Locusts	Do not steal.	Horse Gate
Darkness	Do not lie.	East Gate
Death of firstborn son	Do not covet.	Inspection Gate

Where are you? Are you separated from God with blood in your veins? Are you focused on this world and the way it does things? Are bad choices and ideas covering your life like swarms of flies covering the land? Do you continue to want more and more—never feeling satisfied—more possessions, more control of your life, and more power to live however you want? Are you separated from people who care about and want to help you? Why is it so hard to accept help and change? Is your life falling apart because of all your bad choices? Have you lost everything, including your hope? Are you at that point of giving up altogether? You're still alive. Give up on yourself and how you live, become a living sacrifice, and put your faith in Christ. God loves you no matter where you are or what you've done. Turn to him.

Have you put your faith in Christ? Have you done anything else? Are you following Jesus? Are you learning straight from the mouth of God? Are you learning through trials? Has God taken sin out of your life? Have you been filled with the Holy Spirit? Is the Holy Spirit leading while you are just following him? Are you battling Satan? When we become Christians, many of us stop there. But that is only the beginning of a new life. Continue to press into God, grow closer to him, and constantly talk with and learn from him.

CHOICES

In the beginning, I talked about what influences our choices. Our five senses influence our subconscious mind. Our subconscious mind influences our conscious mind and gives us the ability to make a decision. Every moment of every day, we have a decision we need to make. With all the evil around us and Satan and his demons tempting us, lying to us, and tricking us, it's hard to make the right choices. But when we put our faith in Christ and receive the Holy Spirit, we gain a brand-new influence. God influences us directly. God quiets Satan and his demons, guides us, teaches, gives us peace and rest, and answers our prayers.

God is not a genie in a bottle giving us everything we wish for. God knows what is good for us and will help us, but be careful what you pray for. I prayed for patience one time. The next day at work, I had to train a new guy who was very slow, and he could barely do the job. Do you want a big house, a nice car, and a lot of money? God might give you the opportunity to receive all of those. But you will have to do the work that accompanies receiving them. God is your father and your friend. He loves you and wants to give you many blessings. Listen to God's influence, receive his blessings, and allow him to help you through this life. Walk through the gates of life. Turn away from evil influences, from sin, from Satan himself. Turn toward Jesus, learn new things, have a better life, and experience total bliss in heaven. The choice is yours and yours alone. Make that choice, take that step, put your faith in Christ, and walk through the Sheep Gate.

About the Author

Brian knows what it's like to hate yourself, hate your life, and have no idea how to change anything. He also knows what it's like to feel content with life, have no worries, and want to help others. His main reason for writing this book is to help others have a life they enjoy, Not a life they are forcing themselves through. Whether you're forcing yourself to wake up each morning or forcing yourself to be a perfect Christian life can change and get better. Brian has experienced both of them and with one choice God has changed everything and made it better.

Printed in the USA
CPSIA information can be obtained
at www.ICGtesting.com
LVHW021749061023
760227LV00013B/773